The Making of a King

a King

Michael B. Brown

Yesterday Press (Lifetales Media) * Jupiter, Florida

The Making of a King

© 2021 Michael B. Brown. All rights reserved.

Yesterday Press, (Lifetales Media) 2021
www.yesterdaypress.com
Jupiter, FL
kyvonnehamilton@gmail.com

Cover Design: Karen Yvonne Hamilton

Editing & Layout: Karen Yvonne Hamilton, Lifetales Media.

ISBN: 978-1-7347858-3-8

Dedication

This book is dedicated to my beautiful daughter, Essence Brown. She continues to be my primary motivation as I strive to be a quality example for her to follow.

Contents

Introduction

"I hate having to do this," the judge said prior to sentencing me.

I thought, "If you hate the fact that you have to sentence me so much, then don't and we can all go home." But of course, that wasn't an option, and as much as it pained me to admit at the time, I deserved to be punished. And I was.

"You are hereby to be confined to a Virginia State prison for a total of 82 years with 51 years suspended," the judge continued. This left me to serve 85 percent of a 31-year prison term since the state of Virginia no longer has parole.

Immediately after the sentencing, the judge looked me in the eyes and expressed the displeasure he felt in having to send me to jail. Without seemingly an ounce of remorse, he then proceeded to give me the maximum amount of time he could within my sentencing guidelines. The man was screaming out so many numbers that my family and I got confused, and it wasn't until I got back to the holding cell that my lawyer was able to explain that I got 31 years.

To be real, it still didn't really hit me then because at that point, everything appeared to be happening so fast that it all felt like a really bad dream. But a dream it was not and born a criminal I wasn't. There were several factors that played a role in my being incarcerated. Yet when it comes time for you to be held accountable for your crime or crimes, those factors never get factored in; they only want to know whether you're guilty of that which you were accused, and sadly, sometimes your guilt doesn't even make a difference.

Once that critical question (guilt or innocence) can be answered, they lock you up and throw away the key.

But in most cases, things aren't what they appear to be, and for every cause there is an effect. Every person behind these walls has experienced something that shaped their perspective, and therefore influenced their decision making. If you've ever had the opportunity to speak personally with someone who has been incarcerated, you would see that in no way, shape, or form is my situation unique.

I share my story in hopes to help, heal, and inspire many.

May God bless every word.

CHAPTER 1

"Behold, A Star is Born"

There once was a man by the name of Bernard Brown who had a strong desire to have a son that would/could carry on the family name, much like a king who needs a son to be the heir to his throne. Because of this desire, and him having no luck on his own in this particular area, he decided to petition the help of the Lord. He began to pray faithfully for a son. Throughout the process of him praying and waiting patiently for God to answer, God spoke to him and asked if he wanted a son by the "will" of the Father (God) or by the "will" of the flesh? Because, as we all know, timing is everything. My father's response proved to be a righteous one, and he chose to submit to the perfect "will" of God, even without knowing how long the promise would take to come into fruition.

From there the only question became what to name me. Because in my experience, as you'll soon see, when God acknowledges that your prayer has been heard and will be answered, then you can trust that what you've asked for you will receive. So, with my father having complete confidence in God, he and my mother began to ponder individually about what my name should be. Now the exact timing I'm not really sure of, but I do know that throughout the course of my mother's pregnancy, God revealed to my father the name He had predestined for me, and it was nowhere near what either of my parents had in mind. According to my understanding, my father wanted me to be named Bernard Jr., which would have been a great honor because I consider my father to be a great man, and my mother wanted to give me some white boy's name, which we won't ever mention again.

Please don't look at me that way because we all know that there are certain names that are generally attached to a particular race of people, and then there are names that are generally considered neutral, at least where I came from. But getting back to the point, my mother and father had their plans, and God had a few plans of his own. Whose plan won out? Thankfully, God's did; my father was instructed to name me Michael, and as a testament to my father's greatness, he was obedient in doing so he was able to give me his first name as my middle name as somewhat of a consolation prize, which I think gave him peace about not being able to name his first and only son after himself. It's beautiful how gracious God is in working with us even though in his sovereignty He doesn't have to do so. He even went as far as "visiting" my mother in her alone time in prayer, revealing to her that I would eventually be the star of the family.

You see, God could have just spoken to my father and left it at that, but he wanted to also confirm the revelation he had given my father to my mother, to ensure that she would be onboard as well. Because it takes a village to raise a child, and the Bible says, "How can two walk together unless they agree?" Two perfect examples would be Abram and Sarai, the birth parents of Isaac, and Joseph and Mary, the birth parents of my Lord and Savior, Jesus Christ. God sent messengers to the male and female both to ensure that they would stand and proceed in faith together through the difficult road ahead, and in doing so showed his grace toward them and his strong desire to see them succeed. So, with my mother and father on the same page, June 16th, 1984 marked the day that God saw fit to bring forth a child into this world who had the potential to impact the lives of many, but who would have to travel a long arduous road in order to do so.

My childhood started out really no different from your average middle-class American, although I don't think that financially we were considered middle-class. I was born into a two-parent household where I was free to be a child without ever having to worry about what I was going to eat or whether or not I would always have a roof over my head. I remember birthdays being celebrated with other cousins my age, I remember receiving "big wheels" for Christmas, and I remember running around terrorizing my little sister with this baby doll that talked (this was in the mid-eighties when such inventions were fairly new). Life was pretty good for about the first three and a half years I'd been living. We would often take trips back and forth to Sanford and Orlando, Florida because that's where the bulk of our family resided, and never was I faced with anything that could have the potential to derail me from the path that God had predestined for me. Nor can anything outside of me keep me from my destiny, but of course, I didn't learn that lesson until much later on. I bring up the fact that I never encountered any negativity or experienced any harm to emphasize that because of this fact there was never any reason for my mom or dad to be overly protective of me around these people who were my kin. That's especially critical for me to say because I for so long blamed them for the emotional and psychological trauma I was experiencing.

This situation in which I am speaking destroyed the faith I had in them as my guardians and/or protectors, not to mention pretty much ensured that I wouldn't trust anyone again for years to come. The day of the incident started just like any other day, in that the kids would wait for the adults to get up to make breakfast, we'd eat, get ourselves together, then go out and play while the adults enjoyed their coffee while discussing their plans for the day. In fact, it was such an ordinary day that I don't really remember anything that went on outside of what happened to me later that night. At this particular aunt's house, whenever it was bedtime, the adults (who generally stayed up later than us, especially when they hadn't seen each other in a while) would gather in the living room to enjoy a film of some sort (mostly The Temptations, Five Heartbeats, or The Last Dragon, from what I remember), and all the kids would be sent to the garage, which had been transformed into a bedroom to go to sleep. Of course, we'd play sleep initially to convince our parents that we wouldn't be in any trouble, then we'd pop back up and continue our play. But, inevitably, we always fell asleep and would normally stay that way until sunrise.

But on this particular night, I was awoken in the middle of the night by an older cousin of mine whom I wouldn't say I had a close relationship with due to the age difference, but who I trusted just the same. Upon him realizing that I was now awake, he proceeded to ask me "if he could put his penis in my butt." Me being half asleep, only 3 or 4 at the time, and not even really understanding what he meant by what he said, I regrettably agreed, and before I knew what was going on, I was lying face down with my pants pulled to my ankles with him grinding on top of me. Thankfully, he really didn't know what he was doing, so no penetration occurred, just the experience alone was enough to cause me to feel shame and create insecurities in me that I'd have to battle with the majority of my life.

Somehow my mom found out, but very little was done in the way of helping me or my cousin. Because it's obvious that he had been through something as well; there's no way that, at that young age, you know certain things about sex unless you've seen them done or they've been done to you. My family has historically been the type to handle all discrepancies internally, which isn't a bad thing if you actually "handle" the situation internally. But from what I've seen and experienced in the past, our particular way of handling things which are deemed to be disgraceful, is to simply act as if that person no longer exists or as if the offense never occurred, and that's harmful for everybody. So, the most my family did for me was assure me and my cousin never crossed paths, which I can't say was totally insignificant because as I continued to grow older and became more infuriated by the mere thought of what had been done to me, I had made up in my mind that if the opportunity ever presented itself, I would kill him. But outside of them keeping us apart, I was basically forced to fend for myself, and as you can probably imagine, I had no knowledge of how to cope with the mix of emotions I was forced to deal with, no answers to the questions I was afraid to ask. Just me, a young child attempting to understand why life seemed so bad, why, with a world full of superheroes, there was nobody to save me. Where was my mom and dad when I needed them most?

These are just a few of the thoughts and questions that plagued my mind as a result of the first time I was molested, but to add insult to injury, I was taken advantage of by a heavyset white girl, who had to be at least in the ninth or tenth grade, while riding the bus home from school. I attended a Christian School in West Palm Beach, Florida, which carried all grades from kindergarten to 12th. At this particular time, I was at least five years old and in the first or second grade. I apologize if I seem to be uncertain about a few of the details, but that's simply because for the majority of my life, it's been my mission to block these memories out of my mind. For those of you who have been through a traumatic experience, I know you understand, and for those who have been blessed not to, I ask and pray for your patience in advance. It's amazing how something you've gone through, that you've buried for what feels like forever, once you finally decide to dig it up and address it so the healing process can begin, those wounds almost feel like they happened yesterday. The experience with the white girl lasted about a year, and the sequence of events would generally go as follows.

◈

CHAPTER 2

Early Years

Normally, she and I would be one of the last ones to get dropped off, leaving the bus empty around the time she would "summon" me to the back. Which is mostly where she would position herself in anticipation of our ronda vu. I'm striving to make light of the situation, but clearly it's not funny. Anytime an adult destroys the innocence of a child, there should be severe consequences behind it. Hopefully, I didn't offend anybody with the "ronda vu" joke. Once I reached the seat she was in, she would tell me to sit down, and then she would slide down in the seat, so as to not be seen by the bus driver. She would then lift up her shirt. I was taught to pleasure her in a host of different ways, and tongue kissing, which if I had to pick, was the worst part, due to her not having good hygiene. Needless to say, sex became something that I was made aware of and became interested in at a very young age, so much so that I began to view women (well, girls at that time) as nothing more than sexual objects.

I never told my mother or father what was happening to me during my bus rides home, nor did I ever feel the need to. Contrary to the incident between me and my cousin, "messing around" with the high school girl felt quite natural to me, and towards the end, I actually began to enjoy it. But like I said earlier, it only lasted about a year because I kept getting into trouble at this particular school. I don't know whether the school kicked me out or my mom got tired of them calling her up there to talk about my behavior, but my mother finally decided that I needed a change of scenery. So, I ended up switching schools. A local elementary was the next stop, and at this school, I'd say I did rather well. It was another predominantly white school (not as bad as the Christian school though.) So, I never really felt comfortable, but at the same time it was a great school with great teachers and programs. Which I believe is precisely why my mom signed me up.

I must say that early on, my mom made it a priority of hers to see to it that me and my sister received a quality education. And for that effort, I applaud her. I flourished at this school, as God gave me an incredible aptitude to learn basically anything that was presented to me. I would absorb it all and be almost able to teach it if called upon. Which is the case for a lot of kids at that age, although some to a higher degree than others. I've heard that we're all born with genius capabilities, but somewhere along the way, we reach a "fork in the road" where we either choose to remain focused and/or dedicated to learning, or our interests are diverted elsewhere. This is why they (the school system) provide kids who come from low-income housing with free breakfast and lunch, because if a child or young teen is hungry and worried about where their next meal is going to come from, then obviously they are distracted from the lesson that is being taught.

I know this may seem a bit off topic but bear with me because I said all that to say that while I never had to worry about where my next meal was going to come from (thanks to my wonderful parents), sexual activity became my "new hunger", aka my distraction. Although it took until I was about 11 or so before it really became a problem, up until then, my grades were exceptional. Not that nasty thoughts weren't on my mind prior to then, but lack of opportunity due to the girls my age not being as experienced as I was, nor sharing the same lustful desires I possessed, is really what kinda kept me on the "straight and narrow". Outside of the white girl I lost my virginity to, yes another white girl, which is far more socially acceptable these days then it was in the early 90s, to be real I took a lot of flak for dealing with white girls up until college, so up until 2003. And ironically it wasn't from white folks, it was the sisters that really couldn't stand it, something about all the good black men getting rich then leaving them for white women when they were the ones who originally held them down. Sounded as if they were bitter to me, but who am I to judge? I didn't know what all that meant at the time, but now I guess I can see why they feel the way they do. Even with that being said though, I don't believe a man or woman, when looking for love, should limit themselves to those of their own race. Uniquely we all like who and what we like, and nobody should be judged for their particular dating preference, whether gay, straight, white, black, brown, or yellow. Just my two cents.

But getting back to Shawty that basically turned me out, she was in the 8th and I was finishing off the fifth grade. I've always been tall for my age, so older girls always assumed I was older. If you're wondering what drew her to me, maybe it's the fact that I've been handsome since birth ha. You decide. Regardless of what the young lady's motivations were, I usually slayed them without thinking twice, and this situation was no different. But what was different was the things she did to me and had me do, most of which I was originally going to keep a secret, but I figured Usher set the perfect example when he created the album *Confessions* because he said that "if he was going to tell it, then he might

11

as well tell it all." So, in order for you to feel what I felt, I have to give it to you blood raw.

We met through her dad who was my Little League football coach; she was a cheerleader for another team at the time, but because she cheered and had games and practices as often as we did, we crossed paths quite often. She took a liking to me, and I took a liking to her. We had my younger sister, who was a cheerleader for my team, to set it up where it appeared that Shawty was coming over to hang out with her when in all actuality, she was there for me. We were all in my sister's room when it jumped off; it started as most sexual encounters do, with us making out, and then she began to perform oral on me. Till that point I hadn't experienced what oral sex felt like, but once I did, there was no turning back. I was officially hooked. Not on her of course, although I must say that she served me very well, but on the act itself. She was my first in every major sexual category. It was a onetime thing, and we never really hung out much after that.

Was it me? Was it her? Who knows? But it was definitely fun while it lasted, an experience that I wouldn't change for the world, and that I owe all to my lil sis. She's always been cool like that though, and partly because of that I grew to view her as much more than my lil sister; she was also my friend. I loved and appreciated her then, and I still love and appreciate her now, probably even more so now because she still takes time out of her busy schedule to drop me a line. I don't think she or my family knows how much that truly means to me, even though I strive to express it as much as I can.

But the reason I said that I wouldn't change that experience with the cheerleader I lost my virginity to was because (1) she was super cool and patient with me as she guided me along, and (2) that experience gave me the confidence I needed moving forward. Which is something I lost after what happened between me and my cousin. I became extremely insecure when I came into contact with girls I was attracted to. I was going to use the phrase, "When I was around a beautiful girl," but I thought that would send the wrong message because I believe all women are beautiful. Not to get too religious or deep on you, but if they were created by God ,and God doesn't make mistakes, then they are perfect just as they are - God's masterpiece. I wish more women would develop this perspective about themselves and each other, because then the way they carry themselves would change, and the respect they command from us men would be greater. Because in my experience most men treat women the way they act, that's why guys come up with or adopt words like "thot," "ho," and "busdown," because they are attempting to describe a certain type of behavior. Even me being a little more understanding and less critical of the female species, and someone who doesn't use these words, I still pass judgement in the form of whether this woman possesses the qualities that I'd like to see in my wife, aka is this someone I could take home to meet my parents? And this was way before I ever even considered the notion of settling down. That's just kind of how guys are; even though we say we're just looking for a good time (which on the surface may be true), subconsciously your character is being scrutinized. Sorry, that's just how it is.

CHAPTER 3

Confidence

But back to the story, as I was saying I lacked confidence. And to give you an illustration of what I mean, I'm going to take you back to Orleans Court, a neighborhood I lived in while attending S. Christian and K. Elementary. There was a gorgeous redbone who lived there and went by the name of Coco. I had the biggest crush on her, yet I was terrified to even speak to her. She was older than me of course, that's kind of how I liked them, but I'm sure you're starting to see the pattern. That's why I'm such an advocate for individuals taking the time to examine themselves internally to discover the root causes of why you do the things you do. Regardless of your walk in life, you didn't become who you are overnight; there were influences and experiences that helped shape your perspective. Think about it.

So, in an attempt to gain the affection of Coco, I wrote her a note (I can't even remember what it said), but since I was so young, it probably was as simple as, "Do you like me? Yes or no." I'm much better with words now, but back then not so much. I put the letter in her apartment door, knocked on it, and ran to my big homie Jimmie's crib to hide out. We did what we always do over there, basically just chilled, and that went on for probably an hour or so before Coco popped up with the letter in her hand searching for me. Once she

14

located me, what do you think I did? I wish so badly that I could hear your guesses, but for time sake and to avoid losing you, I'll give you a clue, it's what Usain Bolt is famous for. Yep, you guessed it, I ran. I can't begin to tell you how embarrassed I am to have to admit that to you, even more so than the whole molestation situation, which I have been embarrassed about for the majority of my life.

I know, to many of you, that may sound crazy, but let me explain. Since middle school I've been the ultimate ladies' man, what most might refer to as a "playa," "pimp," or a connoisseur of beautiful women of all ethnicities, which is a title I had grown extremely attached to. For so long it had become my identity, along with being a star athlete, but the former I enjoyed much more, and in my opinion I was a lot better at it. "How can that be?" you ask. Well, even though I was a dominant force on the football field, I still had flaws, areas I could improve upon, but when I was in my zone and locked in on my desired target, my game came off as flawless. I know my wife is definitely rolling her eyes at me as she reads this, but in all actuality, she knows I was a "playa" back then, and still am now; I've just learned to channel all my energy towards her. Now that which I choose to share with the world, is now reserved solely for my queen. But enough kissing up; I'll make it up to her later. I have to tell you the outcome of my pursuit of Coco because I know you're dying to hear it.

So, she popped up, and I ran like a 2-strike convict with the police behind him trying to avoid his 3rd strike; it was as if I had seen a ghost. To be honest, I don't even remember where I ran to; I just wanted to be anywhere but there, which is ironic because the one girl I wanted to be a part of my world, I couldn't even reside in the same room as. I mean what did I actually think was going to happen once she read the letter? Or better yet, what did I hope would happen?

This was a perfect example of someone (me) making an impulsive decision without counting the cost, which is actually the story of my life. I've always been an impulsive person and someone who would fly off the handle if at any time I felt disrespected. I was led by my emotions, anger being the driving force behind the majority of my actions. And my anger issues derived from what happened between me and my cousin, which is what created the insecurities in me, and these insecurities made me feel as if I had something to prove as far as my manhood was concerned. Which goes back to what I said about the experience of me losing my virginity to the older cheerleader giving me a much needed confidence boost. Of course, it didn't completely solve the problem, because anytime you seek affirmation from anything or anyone outside of yourself, you are travelling a dangerous road. As the saying goes, "If you live for their approval, then you'll die from their rejection," and that's the place I was in until I reached the age of about sixteen. Up until then, I was fueled by the praise of men/women, which is one of the reasons I think I fell in love with football and sports in general.

Naturally, with all the anger boiling inside of me, God in his infinite knowledge knew I would not survive without some kind of outlet, a way to vent my frustrations constructively. So, he placed an older individual in my life by the name of Jimmy (the same dude whose house I ran to after putting the letter in Coco's door). I met him because my mom and his mom were good friends. Jimmy was someone who developed a fondness for me, as if I were the little brother he'd always wanted. And on my end, I admired Jimmy; he was strong, athletic, and what looked to me to be the epitome of male confidence. So, in an attempt to be accepted by Jimmy, I would do whatever he asked me to, which was never anything harmful. He could have easily taken advantage of my admiration for him and had me doing all kinds of stupid stuff that could have gotten me into trouble, but he never did. And for that I tip my hat off to him; Jimmy was a standup guy, and someone I wish these gang leaders could meet and strive to emulate, because the direction they have these young guys headed and the missions in which they send them on are far from righteous and will only lead to them spending a lifetime behind bars, if they don't get themselves killed first.

But we'll discuss more about that later in the book.

CHAPTER 4

Sports

So, during one of the times I was tagging alongside Jimmy, we came across a group of kids in our neighborhood, young and old, boxing in the middle of this patch of grass they had set up like a ring. It's amazing how creative and resourceful kids can be when they have their heart set on doing something. At that time, boxing was a sport I was unfamiliar with. I knew tennis because my older sister would often take me to play with her, then get frustrated with me due to the fact that I would treat the tennis balls like they were baseballs and knock them over the fence. Our tennis court in the neighborhood was fenced in, and I'm pretty sure she was tired of having to go and get the balls. Or maybe I went and got them; I really don't remember. Either way, me launching the balls like I was in a home run derby led to us not playing as often as I would have liked, but that was the first sport I can remember playing.

As I watched the other fighters go at each other, I have to admit that something inside of me made me wanna do it too. The sheer brutality of it all sparked something in me, and from that day forward, I was hooked. And this was before I even got my turn to step foot in the ring; it was like something divine spoke to my heart saying this is what you were created to do. But of course, we all know that we can love the idea of something and not be able to handle the reality of it. And if you saw my first fight, you might be tempted to apply that philosophy to me.

My first fight went like this: I tell Jimmy I wanna fight, I get in the ring, gloves on, without an ounce of fear and ready for war, only to almost get knocked out within the first two minutes. I can laugh about it now because I've yet to lose a one-on-one fight since, although those particular fights weren't governed by any rules the way a boxing match would be, so it's a bit different. The kid I fought was nicknamed Donkey Lips, and he was three years my senior, so as I reflect back on the whole setup, I'm starting to wonder why Jimmy put me in the ring with him anyways. Maybe he didn't love me like I thought. Naw, like I said earlier, Jimmy was a standup dude and the reason they matched me up with Donkey Lips, even with the age difference, was because we were similar in size (I've always been tall for my age). He was just more experienced and knowledgeable than me in the art of fighting.

But that experience, like everything I've gone through, only made me stronger. Now I'm a mix between Iron Mike and Pretty Boy Floyd.

Despite suffering my first loss in what could be considered my first fight ever, I still had love for the sport, so my next step was to figure out how to convince my mom to sign me up for it. If you knew her, you would appreciate the difficulty of the task that was ahead of me. But anyway, there was a boxing/kickboxing class right down the street from our apartment that we'd pass at least once every day, so every time we passed it I would bring up the fact that I desired to learn to box. It's been so long now that I don't remember what her initial response was, but her actions showed that she wasn't really fond of the idea because she chose to sign me up for karate instead. Which wasn't all bad, but it's just not what I wanted. I never really asked her why she chose that route, but I've always assumed it was because karate encouraged principles such as discipline and self-restraint, and she probably assumed boxing would turn me into a violent animal. But for that I didn't need boxing; life was already hard at work on me. I gave it a shot though and worked my way up to a green belt before my eyes began to wander and eventually found a new home.

And that new home was on the football field. One Saturday my mom took me to a friend of hers son's game, and just like the day I stumbled upon those kids boxing, I experienced that same adrenaline rush when I watched the collisions that were taking place on the football field. He played flag football at the time, but his older brother played tackle, and those were the games I liked to watch, so as you can probably see, anything that had to do with hitting and/or hurting people, I was pretty much down with. And that's because I was hurting inside, with absolutely no knowledge of how to go about getting better. So, being so young, football and fighting were how I coped with the memories of what I had gone through. Later I would add a heavy dose of sex, drugs, and alcohol to the equation. At that time, the less I was left to my own thoughts the better, at least so I thought. So, upon me asking, my mom signed me up for Little League tackle football that very next season.

I still remember the excitement I felt going out to buy cleats, a mouthpiece, and any other accessories I thought were necessary to either protect me or add to my swag. And what I couldn't buy, I stole, because it was said that a star player had not only to perform like one, but also be the best dressed. So that's why the excess of wristbands and tape on our shoes was deemed necessary because we were attempting to look the part. Also take into account that this was about the same time that I became a fan of the greatest cornerback ever to lace up a pair of football cleats. Mr. Primetime himself, Deion Sanders. Deion had all the young football players chasing after the number 21 and high stepping every time they broke free from the defense. In our eyes, he epitomized what a star should look like, so we emulated that. But a star my first year I was not. I played defensive end (which was not as sexy a position as it has blossomed into in today's game). I wore number 55, and I barely knew the rules. It wasn't until year two that I began to show signs of becoming the star of the family that God had told my mother I would be.

Consequently, my first year playing football is really a blur. I couldn't tell you how often I played or even how many tackles I had, yet every year following I can remember every detail. Even those details that don't matter. It was as if football really didn't start for me until I was thrust into the limelight. I believe God, in his infinite wisdom (as you'll hear me boast about often), hand-picked my team and coaches because he knew exactly the guidance I would need in order to jumpstart my short but successful athletic career. The prep team I played for was well coached, and I say that not only because they realized and maximized the gift that God had given me, but because I admired how they dealt with those players that weren't stars. They did their best to make everyone feel as if they were a part of the team no matter how minimal of a role they played. We were all family, and to my recollection, there was never a race issue. Now that I think about it, it is probably what prepared me to be open to the advances of the white women I've come across in my life (attending S. Christian and K. Elementary also helped).

I never really saw color while growing up. Well, of course I *saw* it, *recognized* that there was a distinct difference, but I never really paid attention to it. Simply because I wasn't trained to notice race as a child; I've developed over time all the stereotypes and prejudices that I have. I wasn't born a racist (which none of us are), and I wasn't raised to be racist. Now that I'm an adult, I can see these prejudices or stereotypes for what they really are and choose not to allow them to affect the way I treat those around me.

It was in my second season that I met the young lady I lost my virginity to, and the year I fell in love with the applause and admiration of men/women. The more they gave me the ball, the more touchdowns I scored, and the more praise I received. I loved hearing how great I was (like we all do), and early on, I especially appreciated it when it came from the male figures/role models in my life. There is no secret that most young boys desire to know and have a relationship with their father, and inevitably it was no different for me. I loved and admired my father deeply and wanted nothing more than for him to be proud of me. And in my mind, sports were my way of doing that. If I played hard, performed well, and got my name mentioned enough then I would be worthy to be called his son. For the record, my father never said or did anything to insinuate that I had to earn his affection, so me striving to do so was solely based on my lack of understanding of how he expressed love. You see some people are vocal with their "I love you's," and some allow their actions to speak for them. My father chose the latter, which as I've matured, I've grown to appreciate all that he did in order to help provide for our household. But as a child, I needed him to be more vocal because of everything I was dealing with inside (my insecurities). That really changed everything as far as our relationship was concerned because I unjustly blamed him for so much when I was growing up. And all the while he didn't have a clue.

So, because of my insecurities and me feeling I had to prove I was a man, I desired, and needed to hear, that I was special, powerful, loved, and a host of other adjectives that would have helped boost my fragile confidence. My dad was my hero growing up, so that's why I speak of the desire I had to obtain his approval. Anything he would have said to me could have had the ability to change the direction of my life. And when I say that I mean anything he said while I was a child, because once I got old enough to think for myself, the negative influences had such a hold of me that there was nothing anyone could have said or done. As a testament to how much of an impact his words had on me, I still remember and often reuse phrases that he used when I was young, such as, "the early bird catches the worm," or "nothing comes to a sleeper but a dream." I often reflect back on how one day when we were riding in the family van together, he was sharing something with me that was obviously weighing on his heart.

Upon concluding what he was saying, he told me, "There will be many times throughout your personal journey where the people in your life won't understand the vision that God has given you, and therefore will be hesitant to support you, and it's in those times that you must learn to encourage yourself."

Pop's, in my eyes, was a spiritual giant; he loved, studied, and strived to be obedient to God's word. He used to quote scriptures to me such as "a wise man uses few words." Sometimes he would even allow me and my sister to stay home and have church with him on Sundays. He became an ordained minister and went as far as pursuing opening his own church. Needless to say, my earthly father was a great man whom God had/has his hand on, and evidence of that was made manifest by how he learned from his own incarceration and turned his life around.

I always wanted my father to attend my Little League games, for the obvious reasons of course. How could I make him proud if he never got to see me play? He never did show up while I played Little League though, and that caused friction between us because I couldn't understand why he wouldn't come. And it frustrated me so much that I decided to speak on it, which resulted in us having an argument where he explained his thought process to me. He figured that as long as he provided the vehicle, gas money, and paid for me to play, it wasn't necessary for him to show up to the games because he had fulfilled his obligation. He also expressed that he never had anyone come to his games when he was growing up, and that's obviously what shaped his perspective when it came to him raising me. At this point in my life, I completely understand because I know all too well how past experiences can affect your decision making, but at that time though, I didn't understand. All I wanted to hear from him was that he'd be at the next game. It honestly took me a while to get over him choosing not to attend my games, mainly because even after I expressed how badly I wanted him there, he still was a no show. In his defense, between my mom (who was always there), and my older brother and sister, I had plenty of people who supported me throughout my athletic career.

So, I was never lacking encouragement. For those people choosing to be there, I should have been grateful, because most kids from where I'm from don't get that. But in my eyes, because of the respect and admiration I had for my father, if all of them had stayed home and he had shown up, that would have been fine by me. He had something that I needed; he possessed the ability to let me know that it was okay to walk with my head held high. Okay to move beyond what had been done to me and truly embrace the limelight, as opposed to shying away from it. But he had no knowledge of what had been done to me. He simply thought that my complaint was solely about him not coming to my games. In all actuality, it was more about him depriving me of that of which I so desperately needed, yet not knowing how to give it to me, as he relied upon the way he was raised. This taught me that parenting is a learned behavior, and if a parent hasn't been instructed in the ways of parenting, then more often than not, trial and error will be how they predominantly learn.

Take myself as an example, being from a two-parent household I have been able to learn from a male and female perspective on rearing kids, allowing me to take the good from both, combine the two, add my own little twist to it, and by doing that, develop my own parenting philosophy. But because of how rough me and my father's relationship started, although he may not have viewed it that way, it took until I eventually got myself incarcerated before I could honestly say that we're in a healthy place. Of course, I've never stopped loving him, and even though in my opinion he was emotionally unavailable, I've learned a lot from him. But personally, it was rough learning to forgive and live with my father.

In spite of my father's absence, I continued to excel in athletics; there were certain unique characteristics that God gave me that I believe caused me to surpass my counterparts in a very short time. One was a lack of fear. There was never a player throughout my little league career and beyond that I was ever intimidated by, or that I would avoid standing toe to toe with. Most would look at me at that time and probably equate my lack of fear with the size advantage I had over most of those I played with, and while for most, that's where their courage would derive from, mine ran a little bit deeper. You see, I believe fear, like racism, is a learned behavior, and I was never taught to be afraid of any man or woman. In fact, I was taught the opposite by those I looked up to, which was to stand your ground no matter what. So those lessons followed me everywhere I went. Big or small, I ran through them all, and I enjoyed every minute of it. In fact, the bigger they were the better, like I said earlier, I quickly fell in love with the collisions, so much so that I often initiated it at times where it wasn't always necessary or there was possibly an easier way. They say that in order to play football at an extremely high level, you have to be a little coo-coo, and along with my God given athletic ability, I had the crazy part down pat. I not only desired to make every tackle, but I was always in search of the next big hit, the kind of hit where you catch someone unexpectedly coming across the middle of the field, and the sheer force of the impact leaves one of you in need of assistance walking off the field. Now that's my kind of collision. Consequently, defense became my preferred side of the ball. Although for my entire little league career and up until the middle of my sophomore season in high school, I played both offense and defense.

⟨≫⟩

CHAPTER 5

Fights

I explained all that to reemphasize how addicted I was, and how prone I became to acts of violence, and how football was a great outlet for me while growing up. But unfortunately, I couldn't play football all day every day, so when left to my own devices, I often argued and fought. Lashing out and rebelling against authority became second nature to me, mostly because I trusted no one, not even those closest to me. So, while growing up, it was difficult for anyone to get through to me because I never genuinely believed that they had my best interest at heart. This is something that I'm pretty sure goes for most of you reading this book because who's going to listen to someone who you don't believe cares whether or not you fail or succeed. No one.

Even before the boxing incident, I was showing signs of aggression when I got into trouble at S. Christian Elementary for screaming in the ear of a young boy who I knew was suffering from an earache. And dig this, the young boy was black. Anybody who hears this story and knows me now might find themselves confused because of the love I have for my people (African Americans) now, and subconsciously always have had. It is too great for me to put into words. But that we'll speak about a little later down the road; it's just ironic that I often felt out of place because of the lack of kids and staff that looked like me, and yet I still chose to terrorize one of my own kind. Which as a side note, basically describes the culture of our communities at this present day. We lie to, steal from, and take advantage of each other while not even realizing that we are fulfilling the role of the KKK, who, because of the progression of American society, is forced to operate in more covert ways, yet their agenda remains the same. And we're playing a prominent role in the continued oppression of our own people. These are the facts.

But like I was saying, the aggressive side of me has always prevailed over the more passive side of me, if that side even exists. Still to this day I have a hard time settling myself down, and it's even reflected in my musical choices. If I can't get hype to it, and it doesn't motivate me while working out, then there's very little chance of me listening to it, and almost no chance of me spending my hard-earned money on it.

My first real fight I remember took place over at a friend of mine's house one summer afternoon. The same friend that my mom took me to go watch play flag football. Our moms were really good friends, so I guess as a way to help relieve each other's stress, they would baby sit for each other from time to time. And so, for me to be over his house was a common occurrence, so much so that I knew a lot of the kids around his apartment complex pretty well. But on this particular day, we were all standing around the basketball court kind of just killing time the way kids do, and me and another kid got into it, and my response was a violent one. We began to tussle around, which led to me getting the upper hand, and because of that and the fact that I wasn't from around there, one of the other kids jumped in. It went from a one-on-one to a two-on-one in a matter of minutes, and even still I held my own.

The kid whose apartment I was over chose to run and get help as opposed to helping himself, which I've never really held against him because there are very few cases where I believe that violence should be a primary resort. And as I've matured I've come to realize that most people, when faced with the choice to fight or run, will take the path with the least resistance. At the core, in my opinion, most people are cowards. I have to admit though that the knowledge of the decision he made that day did play a role, amongst other things of course, in me not taking the initiative to reach out once we began to grow apart.

Even as a child I've never made a habit of holding grudges against anyone, but especially not the people I love, unless the act was viewed as extremely heinous by me. What he did was not heinous, but at the same time, it's difficult for me to ignore what I know, and I think that it would be foolish of me to potentially put myself in that situation again by continuing in that relationship. I feel like far too many of us do; we often get a glimpse of who a person really is and instead of believing them and distancing ourselves from them, we chalk it up to a lapse of judgement. A lot of times it can very well be, but more often than not, it's a part of their character, and that means they're likely to repeat it, so in instances like that, you are never wrong and should never feel guilty for guarding your heart. Trust me, me being a convicted felon, I wholeheartedly believe in second chances and the importance of showing love and/or mercy towards those who have fallen short. But I also believe that in the process of you showing love and mercy, you can potentially become an enabler, and consequently a punching bag, literally and figuratively. Even though I didn't agree with what my friend did, at the end of the day the real problem was with me.

When my mom found out about the fight at my then best friend's apartment, she came and got me, and once home, she threatened me by explaining that if she hears about me getting into any more fights while over his house, I will no longer be to go. At this point in my life not being able to hang out with him meant a lot because I don't believe that there was anyone I was closer to. So, the next time I visited him, I did my best to keep my hands clean (aka to myself) But there were a few older guys there who had seen the fight last time and therefore took it upon themselves to speak on my behalf saying basically that if they hadn't of jumped me, I would have beaten them both one-on-one. Which in my heart is exactly how I felt, but I hadn't expressed that fact to anyone, and nor did I have any intentions on seeking revenge for the unjust act. Now remember my mother's words are embedded in mind, so upon hearing this dude whom I don't even know imply to all those that were in attendance, and most importantly, to the kid that I got jumped by, that I somehow returned to settle the score made me furious. At that point I really wanted to fight him for striving to instigate another altercation, and needless to say he got his wish, because upon hearing him, the kid was more than willing to fight. And on any other occasion, I would have been too, but like I stated earlier, I didn't want to lose my visitation privileges to my friend's house, so I humbled myself and expressed that I didn't want to fight.

If you know me then you know that that was no easy task. Even now at the age of 33, I still find it challenging, yet with the grace of my Heavenly Father I'm a lot better with conflict resolution. Even though I said I didn't want to fight, one of the kids I previously fought didn't want to take no for an answer, so he approached me and punched me in my stomach. I tried so badly not to show how much it hurt but being that he caught me off guard, I ended up curling over in pain. I then tried to walk away, all the while battling internally with the seemingly overwhelming desire to split this kid's head. As I attempted to walk away, the kid followed me, swung, and landed a punch in the back of my head, in which I responded by turning back towards him with my fist clenched ready for war. He paused, which gave my mother's warning to me yet another chance to reiterate itself, and in response to it, I proceeded to head back to my friend's apartment.

I will never forget that experience because it affected me in such a major way, never have I ever felt like such a coward. Upon reaching my friend's apartment, my chest began to ache as if my heart had been snatched from me, and it was as if a bucket of shame had been poured all over my body. From that point on, I made up my mind that I would never allow anyone to disrespect or cause harm to me or the people I love without me doing something about it, regardless of the consequences behind it. And I haven't broken that promise yet. So, for better or for worse, whenever a situation didn't sit well with me, I reacted aggressively. Depending on who it was, I could be verbally or physically aggressive. The target of my aggression is important for me to differentiate because I despise men who beat their women. I know all situations are not the same and that women can themselves be pretty aggressive at times, but for me to agree with any male resorting to violence in any altercation concerning a woman, you would have to convince me that you undoubtedly feared for your life, and that there was no possible way for you to separate yourself from the situation.

But that's just my perspective, I assure you though that I don't offer it without having had my own experiences with crazy women. In fact, there are several instances I can reflect back on where a woman has either struck me or attempted to take my life. One whom is now, and has been for some years now, the mother of my beautiful daughter, Essence. Me and this young lady met at a very young age and because of that I was nowhere near ready to settle down; so consequently, I conducted myself like someone who wasn't ready to settle down, which means I cheated on her as often as the opportunity presented itself, which was quite often due to me being a star athlete and extremely good looking. And understandably, she became infuriated by all the rumors of me sleeping with multiple women. Her response to the rumors was initially (I believe) anger towards them, but inevitably and rightfully it turned toward me.

One day when we were riding in the back of my homeboy's car, she proceeded to strike me. It seemingly came out of nowhere, which left me with no time for a rational response, yet at no time did the thought to hit her ever enter my mind. She wasn't a threat at 5"6" 120 pounds when standing next to me at 6"2" 203. I'll give it to her though, she was extremely strong for her weight and packed a hell of a punch, but not enough to warrant me beating her bloody and possibly ending up in jail. Another example would be this Italian chick I used to deal with back in high school; I think she was a year or two older than me, and when I met her she was still a virgin. This was a huge surprise to me, because how many girls these days actually maintain their purity until high school? Not many where I come from, and they grow up even faster these days due to the Internet. I was already dealing with a chic at the time whom we'll call the one that got away (due to her marital status we will keep her identity concealed), but after learning that the Italian chick was a virgin and noticing that she had access to a vehicle, it appeared to be an opportunity that I thought I couldn't, or shouldn't, let get by me.

Little did I know that beautiful smile was someone who would turn into a girl I'd wished I'd never laid eyes on. But like my daughter's mother, I have to come to her defense because at that time I would say whatever was necessary to obtain what I wanted, whether I sincerely meant it or not. And when you lie, cheat, and seek to manipulate seemingly good people, you garner the kind of reactions I received from the women I've cheated on. So, with that being said, shortly after we met, she ended up giving me her virginity, and as if overnight, she became uncomfortably clingy. I didn't really have too much of a problem with it because at first I wanted to hang around and hookup with her too. Not as much as she did, but I did enjoy her company. Over time though, as is my normal routine, I became less and less interested, and therefore more and more uncompassionate towards her feelings.

Most men will know what I mean by that, because us guys at first (if we care for the person, and genuinely don't want to hurt them) will at least try to hide the dirt that we do, but once we get bored or lose interest in the individual we become bolder in our actions and consequently less discrete. To which I know the women are probably saying, if you care, then why cheat in the first place? And if us men just did right, then there would be nothing for us to hide. Which is an excellent point, and in a perfect world we, men would choose not to stray away from the women we love. But oftentimes our minds don't work like that, and situations that occur are rarely black and white. This is by no means a defense of my actions or the actions of those who cheat, because in my opinion there is none, but simply an observation of we men. We tend to juggle multiple women at a time wishing that each one possessed a particular quality that the other has and vice versa. We do this because, unlike women, we have a hard time expressing what we need from them, and it's a lot easier for us to just go get it elsewhere. All the while we desire to remain with the woman we're committed to. So, to all you women who have a man who loves, supports, and cherishes you, please do not ever take him for granted.

I hear about far too many marriages that end due to the man stepping out on his wife because there is no intimacy at home, their wife has made up in her mind that sex is a tool to be used to manipulate her husband's decisions or should be reserved only for special occasions. Which is the whackest concept in the world to me. If you've got someone who's been down with you through the thick and the thin, then I don't understand how there's anything that that person can't ask of you, provided that their request doesn't violate the sanctity of your union of course, the word "no" should be nonexistent.

So, as I began to lose interest, she began to hear rumors of my indiscretions with other women, and like my daughters' mother, she initially took it out on them. Fighting at football games and wherever else she could get her hands on them, but her fury didn't stop there. She physically attacked me on several occasions, most of which took place after I had decided to let her go. She simply couldn't accept the fact that I had moved on. During these physical attacks, I did all that I could to avoid having to literally fight her as I would a man, and that ranged from me choosing to walk away to me having to physically pin her down until she calmed down. But even though my tactics changed due to the severity of the situation or the lack thereof, the one thing that remained the same was my desire to not harm her at all cost.

Without going into too much detail, I've been in the car with a girl (Dominican chic) on the highway going 100mph with her threatening to kill us both, and even have had a clique of women show up about four cars deep to my homeboys' house to try to jump me because two of the girls out of the clique found out I was sleeping with them both. So, let's just say I know a thing or two about good girls who get raving mad and as a result end up putting you in a position where you could potentially wind up doing something that you'd later regret, or that could land you in prison. I know it can be tough to remain calm in situations like that, but despite that fact, we have to find a way to maintain our composure and handle these situations wisely. How you ask? Well, we can start by acknowledging crazy when we see it and choose to stay away from it. Or avoid putting ourselves in situations like that by loving our partners the way we should. But whatever we choose to do, we got to stop hurting each other.

When it comes to men who rub me the wrong way, my experiences with them are like night and day different compared to women. As I told you before, I had made up in my mind that I'd never let anyone else threaten or disrespect me, those that I hold dearly. And there was never really much talking with me once I interpreted (or misinterpreted) your words or actions to be anywhere near a sign of disrespect. I would explode, and whatever happened after that, just happened. No remorse, guilt, or shame was ever attached to my actions while growing up, it basically was what it was, and I did what I felt like I had to do. And this was regardless of who was around, or the consequences attached to it.

For example, I remember my first middle school fight like it was yesterday. I was in the sixth grade, uncertain about what my middle school experience would be like, but like everyone else, I was determined to make a good impression.

Now when I say 'good impression' undoubtedly most might assume that I mean do good so my teachers would like me or look good so the girls would flock to me. But my teachers and the girls that attended there were the last people on my mind, although getting the girls to flock to me never really required much effort on my part. My initial objective was to solidify myself as someone who is not to be played with. When you think about it, I approached middle school the way most people do prison: draw a line in the sand and make an example out of anyone who crosses it.

So, to kinda set the stage, school was letting out and I had an alright day. I hadn't gotten into any trouble (which was awesome for me, because middle school is where I really started acting out), so I was in a pretty good shape. Of course, I've always been extremely volatile so my mood could easily change at any given moment, but for the time being I was cool. So next I headed to the bus loop and boarded my bus, as is my normal routine, and my normal seat was positioned in the back of the bus. Yes, the back of the bus, after all Rosa Parks and the social activists of her time endured. It's crazy to me how many civil liberties we have now that we don't take advantage of or even think about how people died to obtain them. But I guess that's another topic for another day.

On this particular day though, in typical middle schooler fashion, someone initiated a paper ball fight that, if I'm honest about it, I have to say got a bit out of hand. Paper was being thrown from the back to the front, and vice versa, so as a result, people were being hit that weren't participating in the throwing. And if they felt some type of way about it, they could have sought revenge in a number of different ways that me and the rest of the bus would have been fine with. But this one particular individual, whom we'll call B (only because I can't remember this clown's name), chose to handle his displeasure with someone hitting him in a way that no real street dude could ever respect, told on me. Yes, specifically on *me*. I couldn't understand it. Why me? And most importantly, why tell in the first place? If he had a problem, he could have addressed me directly, yet he preferred the coward's approach to eliminating what he deemed as the problem, me. Because the penalty for such an offense is suspension from riding the bus. So, knowing this and already feeling like he singled me out because I was smaller, younger (he was in the eighth grade), and probably wouldn't do anything about it, I did what I had made up in my mind that I would do to anyone who crossed that imaginary line I'd drawn. I checked him for telling on me and told him to wait until we got off the bus. So, you know how kids do, everyone started chanting "fight fight fight", drawing way too much attention to what was going on. I already had the bus driver on my back cause this rat told on me about throwing the paper, so I'm really trying to lay low in hopes that she doesn't suspend me, other than that I would've beat him up right on the bus.

So, we finally reached our destination and upon us arriving, I saw a police car at a distance, but being that he (the kid who ratted on me) did what he did, and I said what I said, at this point there was no turning back. I exited the bus first, obviously more eager than he, being that he was closer to the front door then me. Or maybe he was simply being cautious and didn't want to risk me getting the jump on him while his back was to me, which I could completely understand, but he appeared to me to be too green to think like that. So, for my ego's sake, we're going to assume he was scared, as well he should have been, because even at that age, you could always look into my eyes and tell that everything I said I meant, and once I made my mind up to do something, you better believe it got done.

So, as soon as I stepped off of the bus, I immediately turned around to face the front door, and as if we were a part of a fight club, everyone gathered around to see if I would follow through with the threats I made. The pressure was on. How I responded in this moment would determine whether I'd spend my entire middle school days dealing with situations such as this, or I'd be labeled as no joke and situations like this one would be far and in between. Which was always the plan: fight so I don't have to fight anymore, then I could focus on those girls. Before B got off of the bus, I glanced behind me to see if the police car was still sitting there. I assumed he was there because fights happened so frequently at bus stops in our area, they figured that their presence would deter individuals like me. And that may have been true, but on this particular afternoon, there was literally nothing they could do. God himself would have a hard time keeping me off this dude.

After I turned back around from seeing where the police car was, he appeared, and before his second foot had a chance to touch the ground, I took off (swung and hit him) on him. He then proceeded to grab me, as I assumed he would, because even though he was older than me, he lacked the experience necessary to defeat a fighter such as me. Not that I was Mohammed Ali or anything, but for my age I was something like him, with the heart of a lion to match.

So, my initial plan worked, and I didn't have to deal with any more altercations that were directly related to me. But as I said earlier, I didn't tolerate the disrespect of my loved ones either, so those issues had to be handled as well. But even as much as I enjoyed violence, I never was a bully (in fact I despised them, and still do), nor did I walk around with the mentality of "I'm going to beat up whomever I come across." While growing up, and even till this very day, you actually have to do something to me, my family, or friends to provoke a reaction out of me. Fighting just for the sake of fighting has never been my thing.

◆

CHAPTER 6

Middle School

Before you anoint me as some kinda saint, I have to admit that once the offense has been committed, egregious or not, I turned into an animal. As you already know, football was the sport I enjoyed the most, since boxing wasn't an option, and being that I was raised in South Florida, I was provided with plenty of opportunities to develop my skills. Sort of like the state of Texas, football in Florida is like its own religion. We play year-round, and those who excel at it get treated similar to gods. As I highlighted earlier, it was this treatment that kept me intrigued and somewhat committed to the sport. I say somewhat committed because outside of football, I had way too much going on, all of which were hindrances to my mental and physical growth. Mentally it affected me because even though I had plenty of street and common sense, the desire to sit in a classroom and be lectured was a desire I lacked, so my academic knowledge began to decline.

Personally, I just never learned well that way (lecture); I learned better by actually doing whatever it was I was being taught. I only was able to muster enough mental energy to show interest in subjects I liked. In order to be successful in high school, and especially the college level, you have to love, or at least value education enough to press through the boredom that comes along with it, and I didn't. My elementary years were great, but once I reached the sixth grade, I just became distracted by other things. I guess I could probably blame it on my increased interest in the girls around me as to why I lost focus academically, but my behavior was starting to worsen as well. I mean my mom spent so much time up at my school that you would have thought she worked there. It's sad but true.

One time it had really took its toll on her, so much so that while she was in the principal's office, she began to cry because she was confused about what it was that was causing me to behave this way. I have to say that seeing her in tears actually hurt me and should have taught me that my actions affect more than just me, but that lesson I wouldn't truly learn until later on. I started off middle school in advanced classes, which shows how much I valued my studies while in elementary, and how sharp of a mind God gave me. I paid close attention to everything that was being taught and excelled at whatever was set before me. But because those that were in my advanced classes didn't look like me, I felt uncomfortable and complained to my mom that I didn't have any classes with my friends, friends that I don't even remember and wouldn't even recognize if I saw them today.

Which speaks to how immature my thinking was, and how foolish it is for anyone to make permanent decisions that will affect their future based on temporary circumstances. I made a decision about my academic future based on how out of place I felt around a large number of Europeans (whites), as if my classmates, school, or level of comfortability would never change. I should have considered myself to be the standard and forced those who grew up with me to rise to it, but instead I lowered myself to their level (academically speaking). I believe my mom ignored my request initially to move into regular classes, but with enough pestering, she finally gave in, and that pretty much ensured that as far as my education was concerned, I'd never really take it seriously again until I got incarcerated.

Once they moved me into regular classes, I began to get into more trouble because what was being taught, I had already learned. Coming from advanced classes, I was what appeared to be light years ahead of my regular classmates. This led to me no longer being pushed mentally, or forced to remain mentally engaged, and that created a lot of idle time for me, time that I often used negatively. Surprisingly, in spite of all the cutting class I was doing, which led to me being picked up by truancy a couple of times, and my acting out in class, I finished middle school with pretty decent grades.

You name it, and I've more than likely done it at some point throughout my middle school career. From skipping class to gambling in the racquetball courts (flipping quarters), going to McDonald's for lunch, or messing around with girls, also in the racquetball courts. I've had sex with a girl in a full classroom while the teacher was teaching, similar to what I used to do with my middle school flame on the back of the bus after basketball games. You see, at our middle school, the boys' and girls' teams used to travel together to away games, due to limited financial resources, I assume. Which makes complete sense because if you're playing the same school seemingly back-to-back, then why would you use two separate buses to get there if you don't have to? The only problem was (if you can call it a problem) that because they chose to use one of those handicapped buses with limited seating, we were piled on top of each other just so we could have somewhere to sit. So, imagine if you can, all that youthful estrogen and testosterone crammed into a minibus. We were all partially dressed because none of us wanted to wear our sweaty uniforms any longer than we had to. Naturally, the curiosity and mischievousness of us kids eventually took over, and immature decisions were made with no thought of the consequences behind them.

For privacy purposes we'll call this middle school flame Suncoast. Me and Suncoast had a really close relationship while growing up, so much so that no matter how much time went by without us having had contact with each other, whenever we did cross paths, it was as if we never missed a beat. She has always done right by me, and any beef we've ever had was due to the mistakes that I made, which is something I can say for basically all the women I've ever dealt with. They all held me down.

◆◇

CHAPTER 7

High School

On through high school I maintained the same level of interest for learning math, science, and language arts that I had in middle school. To be honest I remember everything about high school except how well I did in my classes. I was catered to because I was a star athlete, so being given extra time for assignments that may have been past due was a big reason I was able to remain eligible. Initially, I went to class like everyone else, being a freshman, trying to figure out where I fit into the whole high school scene, and initially I was sure wanting to start off on the right foot. But getting an education was never really a priority of mine; school was always something that we all (me and my friends) did or went to because that's what you were told that you were supposed to do. So, as I think about it, me not being fully committed to someone else's idea or plan for my life is not surprising, knowing me.

So, my high school years went pretty much how my middle school years did, me half ass doing my work, and seeking to sleep with every pretty girl I laid my eyes on, or should I say that laid her eyes on me, because it was very rare that I ever made the first move. Not that I would have known what to say if I did, because pickup lines were never, ever, my strong suit; I was more the type that once you got to know me, it would be impossible for you to keep your hands off of me. Which is why most of the interactions I had with the women of my youth came about because someone introduced us or they introduced themselves, but once the "get to know you" process had commenced, it was nothing for me to keep the ball rolling. Breaking the ice is what scared me the most.

"What scared me most." I know that particular statement may not come off as a big deal to most who read this, but it still blows my mind when I'm able to admit a particular fear that I have or have had, because it speaks to how far my God has brought me. Me refusing to acknowledge what was going on inside of me was the main reason I suffered so much, and for so long. Had I offered my burdens up to the Lord by confessing the emotional pain I was suffering through, I could have been further along by now, in regards to my internal healing process. Because it's not until we acknowledge who God is and that we need Him, that he will then intervene.

Throughout my high school experience, if I did anything, I had fun, and like I said earlier, me being a star athlete, I was able to get away with more than your average student could and was also afforded more opportunities to have a good time due to the popularity I had obtained. Meaning that I was invited to every social event (party) and was shown love by basically everyone in the school, students, and teachers alike. In hindsight this proved to be a blessing and a curse at the same time, because while it made my high school years enjoyable, it also disillusioned me into thinking that everywhere I went I would be, and deserved to be, catered to the same way I was in high school.

Before I go on, I want to explain that I don't in any way blame those who contributed to my disillusionment for any of my failures. I'm just stating that it's a fact that it *did* contribute to my approach to life upon me graduating. And thankfully in spite of me not being completely focused on the academic or athletic obligations I had, I was able to graduate, and even obtain a college scholarship, which was the furthest thing from my mind upon entering high school. My older sister was the first in our immediate family to attend college and graduate, and she eventually became a teacher at the high school I graduated from. Yet in spite of me witnessing the success she had obtained; college was initially never a goal of mine. It only ever became that once I began to receive interest from a plethora of schools lobbying for me to come play football there. Even then it really didn't sink in until I began to take official visits to these schools. Once that happened, I started to see myself possibly becoming the king of a new playground. Sad to say, my mind only ever focused on play, never on the work required to be successful in that arena, so no matter what goals I might have potentially wanted to obtain once I got there, without having developed the necessary discipline to always put business before pleasure, it was inevitable that true, lasting success, would forever elude me, at least in the way that most might strive to succeed in college.

But before I get too far ahead of myself, I never want to make it appear as if no good came out of me having gone through high school. I mean I did meet the woman who would eventually become the mother of the most gorgeous little girl I've ever seen (my daughter), and I also met my ace (best friend), my homie T-black. Not to mention all of the life lessons I learned as a result of me participating in team sports. It's just that at this point in the story, I'm in no way exhibiting and/or practicing the lessons I learned, so until that happens, I refuse to speak on them. As a side note: I believe that's the way every responsible human being should live their lives, only preaching that which they practice, and therefore never holding anyone to a higher standard then they hold themselves.

CHAPTER 8

Virginia Tech

E ven though I was recruited by basically every major collegiate school in the country, the two that I decided to take an official visit to was Virginia Tech University and the University of Michigan. Why those two? To be honest, I really can't tell you, but what I can tell you is that ever since I was a kid, my favorite collegiate school was the University of Florida, so once they offered me up a scholarship, the rest of the schools didn't really have a chance, because in my mind that was where I was going. These other visits were supposed to be nothing more than a free trip, and then I was signing up to be a Florida Gator. Little did I know that God had other plans. None that were directly shared with me because I wasn't spiritually in a position to hear from God at the time, nor would I have recognized it as Him if He had spoken. Most likely I would have responded the way the prophet Elisha did the first two times God called out to him, attributing it to my own thoughts or the influence of someone I knew. So, instead of speaking to me directly, He created a scenario in which He knew I would make the decision that I made.

Now why specifically He wanted me to wind up in Virginia, I cannot tell you, I guess that part will be revealed once my time here is done, but to Virginia I went (by way of Virginia Tech University), and in Virginia I will remain until

God sees fit to release me. You would think that since it was God's will that I went there, that everything as far as my acceptance into the university would have at least gone smoothly, but it was anything but that. Turns out that with my final GPA, it was still necessary that I went to summer school in order to improve on a few grades. So, I go the whole summer in hopes to fully qualify myself for the scholarship that was offered me. Upon completion, under the impression that I was now qualified, me, my mom, dad, younger brother, and my daughter's mother (although she wasn't pregnant then), packed up the van and headed to Virginia Tech.

Only to find out that upon arriving there and attempting to register, that there was some sort of clerical error that was made where my replacement grades from my time in summer school had not yet been approved by the community college I attended, or they had not yet got around to submitting them to the university I committed to. And because of that, me and my family had to sit around for a couple of days without knowing whether or not the enrollment process would ever go through.

During that time, I wasn't allowed to gain access to my dorm room because I wasn't officially a student yet. I wasn't allowed to practice with the squad, but the coaches did allow me to go watch and have access to the practice facility the way any other student athlete would. I have to admit that that helped aid me in keeping my spirits up, because emotionally I was a mess. To be honest, I couldn't really express to you at that time, or now for that matter, as to why I emotionally broke down, but if I had to guess, I would probably say that it was because it was the first time I had ever really experienced failure. I had genuinely set my heart out to do something and didn't accomplish it, so me having been spoiled in that way and finally experiencing the other side of the spectrum (disappointment), my emotions kinda got the better of me.

And just to clear things up, I don't wish to mislead any of you into thinking that I never failed while growing up because that simply would not be true, but to reiterate what I said earlier, I "never failed at anything I wholeheartedly pursued." Even at that age I knew that if you were partially committed to achieving something, then you should expect partial results, so there were several things that I halfheartedly went about and as a result, the goals I may have set were never actualized, and as well they shouldn't have been.

I believe that the reality is based on God's divine plan that all would one day learn to "love the Lord thy God with all of their heart, soul, mind, body, and spirit," meaning with everything that one has, in hopes that that "all in" mentality would carry over into every area of our lives. God in his infinite wisdom set principles in place that if abided by, the individual who humbly submits to them will as a result obtain everlasting success, meaning here on earth, and also in the hereafter. And these principles are designed to help keep us from living beneath the standard in which Christ has called us to, the abundant life that He sacrificed his life so that we may experience it.

But despite all of the obstacles that lay in wait for me, once I arrived at Virginia Tech University, everything did eventually work out and my scholarship and enrollment was finally, officially, given the stamp of approval by those who were in charge of doing such things. So, me and my loved ones went about saying our goodbyes, which was also emotional as you could probably imagine, a momma bear having to release yet another one of her cubs into this wild world we live in to fend for himself. And on my end I was dealing with a mixture of nervousness and excitement.

Nervous because I didn't really know what to expect, and I'd never been that far away from South Florida (home) for more than a week, and excited because as I looked around, beautiful women were all I saw. And this was all before the official freshman move in day, which is a date set by the university for the regular students to go through the exact same process me and my parents went through. Of course, it was hell for the parents, but it was heaven for us.

If I remember correctly, me and the rest of the freshman football class that year strolled around the campus that day perusing the female students that we hadn't met yet, while waiting for their overprotective parents to release them from their stronghold. It was a beautiful fall evening, the type most people would enjoy, and one that once it all came to a close and we went back to our dorms, left me feeling more confident in the possibility that I could potentially thrive there. So, with that confidence, I attempted to try to transform myself into what would be defined as a "student athlete", which by its unofficial definition I believe it to be someone who disciplines themselves in the classroom as well as their arena of play, someone who commits themselves wholeheartedly to their team and studies by only making choices that would increase their potential odds to succeed.

Me personally, I was far too selfish for all that, and by the time I reached college, I really had no interest in the whole getting up and going to class charade. To be real, I just wanted to have fun, and whatever I had to do to achieve that goal, I was all for it. College was just another playground that I hoped I would one day be the king of. Looking back on it, of course I wish that I would have approached the opportunity for me to get a first-rate education and physically and mentally prepared for life in the NFL more maturely, but in 2003, at the age of 18, mentally that's where I was at. And as a result of my approach or attitude toward the opportunity God had graced me with, I did have a whole lot of fun. But I also experienced a whole lot of pain due to the foolish decisions I made, the greatest penalty being the loss of my scholarship.

Looking back, I can now see that all those that were constructively critiquing my behavior, be it getting into fights, showing up late for study hall, or not giving maximum effort in practice, were only trying to drive me to be better. But I've never handled any kind of criticism well, whether motivated by love or not. Plus, I've always had trust issues due to my molestation as a child, so it was impossible for me to believe that these complete strangers somehow had my best interests in mind. And for an individual such as myself, trust is a key factor in me listening to anything you have to say, and even then I only take that with a grain of salt until I'm able to do my own research. And in the end, that process often results in me coming to some type of conclusion. Which is the precise mentality that helped solidify my faith in Christ Jesus, because when everyone in my family was trying to preach to me, instead of just taking their word for it, I decided to search these truths on my own, and once I found what they were saying to be accurate, only then did I surrender my life to Christ.

But I'm getting a bit ahead of myself, because while I was ripping and running through Blacksburg, establishing any kind of relationship with the "creator of heaven and earth" was the furthest thing from my mind. The only relationships I was interested in developing was with my money and whatever fine honey I found desirable, whatever scheme I considered profitable I always wound up involved in, and whatever skirt was down for a good time, she often found herself seduced by me. As far as my success rate with women was concerned, I enjoyed the company of many, but there was one in particular (who shall remain nameless) who eventually stole my heart. Although upon me first seeing and then meeting her, it originated as pure lust. I, for some reason, found her extremely attractive even though she was far from the most beautiful woman I've ever been with. To be honest, I can't really tell you specifically why I was so irresistibly drawn to her, all I know is that once I laid eyes on her, I made up in my mind that I had to have her. Now before going on any further, I want to clarify that in no way am I implying that she was not a pretty girl, because she absolutely was, so much so that your "average joe" probably would have fell in love at first sight, just not a guy like me.

The pursuit was on, and how I was going to get her to notice me was the next question I was going to have to answer, because my past history had shown that once she did notice me, it would just be a matter of time before she realized I was the man of her dreams. Then, after we'd slept together, she later found out I'm not. I know it may sound cruel, but I must be honest, I've caused many women to cry, and as hard as it may be for you, and for them at the time, to believe, I never purposely meant to hurt any of them; I really didn't realize how harmful my lying and cheating actually was, or the impact it would have on them. That's how blinded I was by my own selfish needs.

Before I continue on, I feel led to apologize to all the women of my past for the heartache and pain I've caused each of them. I was a scumbag for my behavior towards you, and I pray that one day you all can find the strength to forgive me. I sincerely apologize.

But in getting back to my pursuit of this young lady, I really had no experience just boldly walking up to women and asking their name, because prior to entering college, that was never required of me. So, fortunately, I had an *in* through a fellow freshman teammate who was trying to court her roommate. You see, that's kind of how my life up until my incarceration worked out, similar to the Greek mythological, legendary King Midas, everything that I wholeheartedly set out to accomplish, I achieved. And everything that I touched turned to gold. In hindsight, I came to realize that even while I was still up to my earlobes in sin, God's grace was upon me, not necessarily aiding me in my sinful endeavors, but holding true to the biblical principle that with enough belief anything is possible. I simply believed that me and her getting together was a full-on conclusion, and it was the power of that belief that began to open up doors that would eventually lead to us becoming an *item*.

The word of the Lord holds true regardless of what situation you apply it to, good or evil, but for true, lasting success it would be in your best interest to apply it to righteous pursuits, because the reign of the wicked rarely lasts long. It took a few visits before me and this young lady hooked up, but once it did occur, we were pretty much hooked on each other. Not that that discouraged me from repeatedly hooking up with other girls, but if someone was to have asked, I would have had to admit that as far as importance to me, she definitely ranked ahead of them all. Hence the reason I decided to even mention her in this book; she was the first woman outside of my family who I ever felt loved me unconditionally, and it was her example of that love that, once I committed my life to Christ, helped me to somewhat understand the love He has for His children. She is one of the major reasons why my faith has gotten to be so strong, and why in spite of my many flaws, I don't participate in self-condemnation because I know how fully and completely God loves me. I owe her a lot, and hopefully one day I will be able to repay the debt that I feel I owe. Until then though, I pray God's continued blessing on her life.

It took a full football season and a couple of months before my foolishness finally started to catch up with me, leading to the head coach requesting to meet with me to discuss my future on his team. I, of course, didn't know what the subject of the meeting would be prior to me showing up to his office, but based on all the rumors that were swirling around about me being involved in this and that, I knew that if the head coach wanted to see me, then it couldn't be good. And as it turns out, it wasn't. He was rightfully disappointed in my performance off the field and elected to take away my scholarship for a semester to see just how bad I desired to be there. It was an attempt to wake me up and hopefully cause me to recognize/appreciate the enormous opportunity that was provided for me by God through Virginia Tech University. If I walked the straight and narrow for that following semester while off scholarship and proved to be the perfect student athlete, then my scholarship would be reinstated.

Even though my probationary period would only be temporary, based on my performance, I couldn't help but feel like my time there was done. I assumed that there was no way my parents could afford to foot the bill for a whole semester of college. Between books, tuition, room and board, then a meal plan on top of all that, I figured it would be far too heavy of a burden to bear being that our lifestyle was far from extravagant. To be honest, at the time that me and my coach were having this conversation, I didn't know how much a semester of college even cost, but we were always taught that only those select few that were extremely "well off" were able to go, unless you played ball like me. So, without even consulting my parents about what was going on, I made an executive decision and told the head coach that me and my family weren't going to be able to pay for a semester on our own, so the conversation ended with us both having the understanding that my career there was pretty much over once the school year concluded.

It wasn't till then that I told my mom what happened, and she expressed to me that I shouldn't have spoken so quickly because we could've possibly figured something out. But in that moment, I was thinking that I was doing what was best for the family by not asking them to add yet another bill to all the others they were responsible for. This was my problem, created by my own doing, so I felt the need to deal with it myself, although how I was going to do so was a question I had yet come up with an answer for. After speaking with my mother and having come up with no solutions on my own, I went back to the coach to express that I did desire to remain there, and my parents were willing to support me in any way imaginable to see to it that that happened. But as I suspected, based on the whole vibe of the previous meeting, my time there was done, and my only option was to attempt to move on.

The head coach confirmed this by saying, "I think it is best if you went somewhere where you'd have a fresh start."

CHAPTER 9

The Good, The Bad, and The Ugly

I understood that and knew that it was well within the coach's right to say that. He had no reason to believe that my behavior would change, and as you can tell by the fact that I'm writing you from prison, it didn't. So, his decision proved to be the right one, and I believe ultimately what God wanted as well because the Bible says that "the heart of the king is in God's hand." If it was the Father's will for me to stay, he could have easily influenced the decision of the coach. Which as you see, He decided not to do, which means that He also felt it was in my best interest to move on and had already gone before me to prepare a place.

Even in the midst of my sin, God never stopped loving, providing, and ordering my steps in such a way that I'd cross paths with someone who could share with me the word of truth. Eventually, when that didn't work, he often lovingly allowed me to fall into difficult circumstances to humble and prepare me to receive His truth. Because there's nothing like falling on your face to get the stubborn flesh of man to finally lay prostrate before the "Lord of glory". As sad as it is to say, most of the time, that's exactly what it takes to bring us to the end of ourselves, so we come to realize that without making Him the Lord of our lives and therefore submitting to the plan He has for us, life is never really going to be as fulfilling as it could be.

I have a little saying that I use when explaining to others why I refuse to turn my back on the "creator of heaven and earth" and it simply goes that "Without God, my life ain't gone go right" (please forgive the poor grammar).

I need Him just to get through the day, because if left to fulfill my own will, there ain't no telling what I might do. And that's just me being real. My mind doesn't work right sometimes, but just like the Apostle Peter, who Christ called out of the boat to walk with Him on water, as long as my focus stays on Jesus, I am able to function at the level God created me to.

I know some of you may be saying to yourself that you rarely do anything wrong or you're "a good person" so for those reasons you don't see the need to commit your life to Christ, because at the end of the day, even though you err at times, at least you're not a criminal. Which sounds like pretty sound reasoning on the surface, but when you dig a lil deeper and come to find out that the Bible says, "that even on our best day, our righteousness is comparable to filthy rags" (paraphrasing), and that no amount of "good deeds" attributed to your life can save you from eternal damnation, your argument begins to crumble a bit.

Christ states in His Holy Word that "He is the way, the truth, and the life, and that no one may come to the Father but by Him." It's impossible for you to save yourself, so Christ came in the form of man to lay down His life so that you might live.

So please, I encourage you to surrender your will and choose to follow Him; the results, I promise, will be life changing.

To reiterate how God never left me even in the midst of my mess, he gave the head coach enough compassion for me (in spite of his disappointment in me) to offer to give me a positive recommendation to whatever school I decided to try to transfer to James Madison University in Harrisonburg, Virginia. It would have turned out to be a really big deal had God not outdone Himself by providing the defensive end coach (which is the position that I was recruited to play at Virginia Tech) with a more prominent position at a nearby school. Since he had coached me for the short time I was at Virginia Tech, he knew what I could do athletically. My situation was still in limbo, and he graciously asked me to come with him to embark on this new journey together. You see, to me, things working out like that have to be God. I mean here I was on the verge of being right back in West Palm Beach not knowing what my next move would be, and seemingly out of nowhere, God provided me with yet another opportunity to get a great education and potentially be the starting linebacker on an extremely talented team.

This was an opportunity that I wish I had had the character to take advantage of because although I had every intention to approach this new situation with a new attitude, it wasn't long before I reverted back to my old ways. Which you will begin to see is basically the story of my life; I fall short or err in some way, then I determine that I'm somehow going to turn over a new leaf, only to wind up doing the same thing I just vowed not to do. They say that the "road to hell is paved with good intentions," and if that's the case, then I was a prime example of someone who essentially had a good heart but often found himself committing the dumbest of crimes.

This is not to insinuate that there is such a thing as a *smart* crime, because choosing to live a life of crime is in and of itself a foolish idea, but if you are going to plot or plan something illegal to do, then let it at least be worth the risk. And by 'worth the risk' I mean the earning potential should be enormous enough that if/when you get caught (because we all do eventually), you can afford your own lawyer, provide for yourself while behind bars, and your family is straight (financially)while you're gone. If you can't cover those three areas doing what you're doing, then you need to leave it alone.

I know that a lot of my Christian brothers and sisters will turn their noses up at that advice, and probably want me to take a harsher stance on crime. But honestly, that's not what this publication is, because although I may not always agree with the decisions my brothers and sisters make, and by brothers and sisters I mean all humanity, not just those who walk, talk, and believe like me, I won't ever conduct myself as if I don't understand. Not to make excuses for myself or anyone else who has chosen the "broad path" that the Bible warns us to avoid, but when times get rough and pressure then gets applied (whether it's by your teachers or the bill man) often times we don't respond the way civilized society would like us to. Our response is then judged and depending on whether our peers view our actions as unforgivable, we are then given a pathway to redemption or ostracized. After everything I've seen, done, and gone through, I can't see myself ever turning my back on those that society deems unredeemable.

So, to the "Pharisees and Sadducees" who would prefer I stone those that Christ also died for, because He didn't just die for you , this book is not for you, but for those who believe that everyone deserves a second chance. I believe that together we can help make this world a better place. My time at JMU, and therefore in Harrisonburg, was definitely bittersweet, due to the simple fact that while I experienced much joy while I was there, I also suffered a lot of pain, largely due to the poor choices I made. I had friends, most of whom were female, although I never really felt at home there. My coach (the one that brought me there) attempted several times to connect with me on a more personal level. Why that was I'm not exactly sure, but I believe that in some way he could relate to being in a strange place around people you obviously don't know and therefore can't trust. Yet all of his efforts were in vain; I just couldn't at that time open myself up to anyone outside of the young lady from Virginia Tech that I previously spoke about, and even with her I held back a large portion of me. Me and the coach probably would have had a better shot of becoming friends if in some way he could have gotten me to see him as more of a peer and less as a coach, because being in the presence of authority figures, especially those that pride themselves on discipline as opposed to exercising diplomacy, always made me feel uncomfortable. Not that he could have known the right approach to take, because I lacked the courage and the knowledge to address the inner turmoil I was experiencing, let alone open up to someone else about the pain I was dealing with.

So, these wounds remained uncared for, and eventually ate away at any opportunity I had at living a happy and healthy life. Self-medicating became the way I coped with the pain, and to be completely truthful, I can't even pinpoint how, when, or where it started. It was as if all of a sudden I was smoking, drinking, and/or popping pills every chance I got. Partying and sleeping with women have always been my favorite pastime, but like the drugs and alcohol, it also began to consume my life. To your average college goer though this probably sounds like a typical semester away from home, but trust me, my commitment to the wildlife closely bordered extreme and might've surpassed it depending on who you ask. And the worst part wasn't that it started to affect my performance on the field or hindered me from acquiring a decent education off of it, but that it kept me from facing *me*.

The good, the bad, and the ugly. I didn't know who I was, where I was headed, or why I was created, basically traveling through life with no direction or purpose. And in order to feel better about living beneath the level I was created for, I surrounded myself with those who either lived beneath their potential as well, or those who wished they had the courage to sometimes live outside of the rules. Those who may not have agreed with my decision making but wasn't confident enough to say anything thought I was cool. My closest confidants though, were those who were in most aspects just like me, at least so it seemed.

But we'll get further into that a little later on. For now though, those relationships served the same purpose as the drugs and alcohol, to distract me. Like I mentioned earlier, I started out good, but shortly after my arrival, my grades began to suffer due to me not going to class like I should've. My performance on the field started to decline due to all the extracurricular activities I partook in (many late nights), and once I failed a few of the random drug test that they gave the student athletes, my relationship with the coaching staff began to fade. Not that we were ever really close, but the gulf between us was really noticeable at this point, even though they gave me more chances than I deserved. I mean honestly, I probably broke the record for disciplinary early morning workouts, which was normally the penalty given for the violation of any number of the team rules. I literally spent so much time running stairs and sprints that my teammates and coaches created jokes about me being one of the fittest athletes in America, which could've one day possibly been true had I not also been drinking and smoking every night. But on the other hand, if I wasn't drinking and smoking, I more than likely wouldn't have been punished in the first place, so maybe not.

When I failed my second random drug test, they insisted that I see a counselor/therapist to discuss why I couldn't seem to stop smoking even though I knew that the test was coming. Of course, I didn't know the exact date or time of the test, but I knew that once anyone failed a drug test, their name was then put on a short list, therefore increasing the frequency in which they were tested. I had never been to a therapist prior to, and never thought that any good would come of me meeting with this one, but there was something about this woman; she was eventually able to convince me to open up. And with all the fun I had, my sessions with her are the only experience that I wouldn't trade.

I literally was able to escape every expectation placed on me by the outside world and was able to just be me for those few hours. And being able to just be me in a world full of rules and regulations was something that if I had to, I would swim across the ocean to obtain, it means just that much to me, as I'm sure it means to majority of you. Who doesn't want to be loved and accepted by their family first, and then their peers?. You show me someone who says that they don't, and I'll show you a liar, not to say that they want it bad enough to compromise who they are or what they believe, but in a perfect world if asked whether they'd prefer to be loved or ostracized, what do you think their answer would be?

The desire to be loved is the strongest innate desire we possess, in fact it's so strong that people do all kinds of unrighteous things to experience even a glimmer of it for a fleeting moment, most of which they later regret and only leave them longing for more. And that type of unconditional love and acceptance I had yet to experience from any adult outside of this counselor (probably because my acting out justified her employment. Whether the adults throughout my life meant for their attempts to chastise me to come off the way they did (as if they didn't love me no matter what) or not I'm not really sure, I can only assume that they meant well. But their approach to discipline without utilizing the mentorship aspect of it left me to misinterpret the message that they were trying to send. It felt as if when I did good in school and was scoring touchdowns and making tackles they loved me, but when I wasn't making wise choices their attitude towards me shifted dramatically.

I know to many that my logic behind all of this may sound a bit insane, I mean you're probably thinking that when I did err in judgement, their attitude should have changed, which is an understandable position, but when dealing with children and/or adolescents, continued punishment without the reaffirmation of the love you have for them will always provoke more rebellion and create a greater divide between you and the child. For example, I had an incident occur between me and my younger brother where he took a few things of mine without my permission and hid them so I couldn't find them, so basically he stole from me. You know how it go, him being my little brother he admired me, so he decided to *borrow* a few things to look like me without asking. But when I discovered that the items were missing, coupled with the fact that I had already been previously informed by my mother that he was going through a sticky fingers phase, I knew that how I handled this situation could positively or negatively affect the longevity of this phase.

So, after much thought, I called him into my room, forcefully grabbed him and slammed him on the bed, then proceeded in a stern voice to express that if my belongings were not where they were supposed to be by the time I returned to the room, we really were going to have a problem. So, I left out, gave him about ten minutes, then returned to find everything back in its place. But as opposed to leaving it at that as if I had accomplished some monumental feat by spooking him into returning my stuff, I took it upon myself to call him back into the room to reiterate how much I loved him and explain why stealing from anyone (especially family though) was unacceptable. And you want to know what he ran out of that room saying to my mom? "Mommy, Michael says he loves me." Not "Mommy, stealing is bad," or "Mommy, Michael's mad at me." All he cared about was that those who watched over him (aka those whom he had grown to love and trust) loved him in spite of his flaws. I believe that it was primarily that experience at such a young age that enabled me to still possess such a strong level of influence in his life. No matter how great the distance between him and I, to him I'm always going to be big bro who loves him no matter what, and hopefully my daughter also will always view me that same way.

In spite of my bad habits and lack of focus on the things that really should have mattered at that time, I was able to make it through the entire fall season without getting kicked off the team, a team that went on to win the 2005 National Championship, which speaks to the talent on that team. Not long after the season started, I found myself in the starting lineup, me and another young linebacker who had similar size, speed, and an eye for the ball, wound up taking the spots of two seniors who were of lesser talent. But what all three of them (the two seniors and the other young linebacker) had that I didn't was a great work ethic, on and off the field, which is something that is absolutely necessary if you plan to be successful in any area of life for an extended period of time.

Raw talent will only get you so far before you're forced to couple that talent with hard work in order to oftentimes just remain in the middle of the pack, let alone be considered the upper echelon of your field. That amount of success requires an insane amount of self-discipline and self-sacrifice, especially in the *wide world of sports*. At the lower levels, such as Peewee League, I was able to coast along without much effort (although I always played hard) because I was bigger and faster than most of the kids my age, and right up until and through high school my size, speed, length, and athleticism enabled me to dominate most teams we faced. I ran like a gazelle, and had energy for days, even while smoking almost every other day. Before and after practice when we ran as a whole, I was able to lap most of the team; at that time, it just didn't affect me. So that experience throughout high school gave me the impression that my body would forever function optimally regardless of what I put in it or did to it. On top of that, I can't remember anyone ever preaching the importance of hard work or self-sacrifice to me or any of my other comrades. Not that it would have changed anything, because as hell bent as I was to do what I wanted when I wanted to do it, there was slim chance that I would have listened anyway.

As I often reflect on past events, I sometimes feel like if the right spokesperson (someone I admired) would have approached me with sound advice about how to be successful in life, then things might've turned out differently. You know that's something we all do, wonder what if, then come up with a host of excuses/reasons (most of which are probably valid) why our life turned out the way that it did. But the fact of the matter is that when you become old enough to branch out into civilized society, and then do something that violates the rules that they have put in place, they can care less why it is you committed the infraction, all that matters is that you did.

Which is what I experienced at both educational institutions (colleges) that I attended, and definitely once I got tied up in the judicial system, nobody really cared why I was so angry, only if they could harness and focus that anger on activities that would hopefully one day benefit them. So once the season was over, I pretty much knew that my time at James Madison University was coming to a close. They had received my final grades and were not pleased, which is why I rarely played in the National Championship game. The coach came up to me on the bus before the game to voice his displeasure and to inform me that I would only be participating in special teams. It was a conversation that only me and him took part in, but I was embarrassed as if he had posted the conversation on a billboard. Which I'm sure was the response that he was looking to get out of me. It's funny though how it takes us as humans to lose something that we love in order to realize how important it (or they) was to us.

I really had a bad habit of this, and only ever appreciated sports when I was told that I couldn't play. Which also pretty much explains my relationship to women up until that point; they were all disposable. I enjoyed them while we were together, but once they left my presence it was out of sight out of mind. Yet now that I'm incarcerated, you can probably imagine how much I miss them. And not just one or two, but at some point throughout my bid, I have reflected on my time with every woman I've ever been with, and at one point made a list just for kicks. Even those that I didn't have the pleasure of sleeping with, they all possessed a unique personality, a flawed beauty, and a specific skill set that made them all special in some way. I thank God for the experiences I shared with each and every one of them, good or bad, and I sincerely pray God's best over their lives. I know they're all probably saying, "It sure is a fine time for you to start appreciating us now."

Trust me, I wish I was more of a gentleman while growing up, but even though I rarely acted like it, I've always considered women to be God's most precious creation, meaning that I'd rather for the sun to burn out and the ocean water to evaporate before I'd want to see the female species cease to exist.

So, we won the National Championship and found our way back to James Madison, soon after an appointment was scheduled between me and the head coach. I know what you're thinking, deja vu right? To be honest, you are absolutely correct, this meeting went almost exactly like the meeting with the Virginia Tech coach. The only difference was that as opposed to refusing to stay and pay for the following semester while striving to earn my way back on the team, this time I consulted with my family and we agreed to give it a try. Which was another poor decision on my part because I knew that the likelihood of me changing anything about my behavior was slim to none, and what's worse is that my parents had to refinance their home to keep me in school (so basically take out a loan), holding out hope that their second oldest son could and would do better.

CHAPTER 10

Charlotte

Unfortunately, I let them down, so the money was wasted literally and figuratively. Literally because I put forth no more effort than I had in the past and ended up not graduating, and figuratively because I at least should have deduced from the gesture that my family had my back and were willing to do whatever it took to help me succeed. While preparing for this unpaid semester, I ended up moving in with a guy whom we'll call *Charlotte*. He was younger than me and someone whom I had grown to view like a little brother. So much so that when we weren't off separately doing our school thing, I took him wherever I went. I mean trips back and forth to Virginia Tech to see my chick and also to put him on with a few of her home girls. I even allowed him to visit my parents' home in Florida. Which is a rarity for me because I didn't even like for people I kicked it with in high school to really come around the house. I just knew that how we liked to party, my parents wouldn't approve. Every so often though my mom would catch me out front with one of the chicks I was dealing with and invite us in so she could meet them; she was always pretty slick about that.

But the point is that for me to invite him to my Florida home, I had to have viewed him as someone I could trust. I loved and treated him like he was family, and at any time, it was second nature for me to come to his aid if he ever needed me. And vice versa. At least so it seemed. When we got wasted, we did it together. When we 'smashed' chicks, we did it together. When we got into drama, we fought together. And when we robbed, we robbed together. So, there was no reason for me to ever assume that one day he would rollover on me to the police. I mean I knew that he had a tendency to panic when pressure was applied, but he always came through, so to find out after all we'd been through that he was testifying against me really caught me by surprise.

But I'm definitely getting ahead of myself, because prior to us even meeting each other, I was robbing and burglarizing apartments all over the Harrisonburg area. To be honest, I had been scheming, scamming, stealing, and robbing since about age 12, which may be news to many due to how discrete I prided myself on being. The only crime you'd probably ever catch me committing out in the open was assault because I had little restraint in the moment when someone disrespected me or those that I love. There was no waiting for a more opportune time, wherever the offense was committed was where I handled it.

So, what I'm saying is that by the time me and Charlotte crossed, I already had a habit of doing whatever I thought needed to be done in order to obtain some extra cash. Of course, the younger I was, the pettier the crimes I committed, because in all actuality, I didn't really need much since my everyday needs were provided for by my parents. So, me choosing to engage in criminal activity was not based on a need to survive, but on the desire I had to look flashy. Whether it was by stealing a pair of shorts to match my track jersey, or a new pair of sneakers and wristbands to play ball in, I just had to be fly.

Which is the mentality of most where I come from; when it comes to sports they say, "If you look good, you'll play good." And in life, "If you look good you attract the ladies." And what young man do you know that while growing up didn't want the attention of the ladies? But beyond just the girls, as I began to get older, the crimes I committed I did more so to support my nightlife, which ultimately became my 'day life' too.

Because after a while, it didn't matter to me what time of the day it was in order for me to get the party started. I enjoyed drinking, smoking, popping Ecstasy, and going out, and I loved to treat those that I loved to a good time. It gave me a euphoric feeling to be able to financially take care of the people around me, and when I couldn't (like most men), I felt like less of a man, less empowered. The fact was and is that I hate feeling helpless in any situation, and I hate having to depend on others to sustain my lifestyle.

It's always been a pride issue with me; I'd much rather be in a position to lend then to borrow. Which is a statement to which I believe most would respond by saying "me too" or "who wouldn't rather lend than borrow"? Because of that you may make the assumption that we are one in the same. But with most, I would have to respectfully disagree, because the extremes to which I was willing to go in order to be/remain the 'lender' and not be the 'borrower' were more extreme than most would go to, which is a good thing at the end of the day. And that actually should provide a glimmer of hope for those who are unsettled about the state of affairs in this country; there are more decent people than there are unruly, and even the unruly are capable of being saved. I mean just look at me.

I experienced a lot during that short period of time between me getting kicked out of school and me deciding to go on a 'robbing spree'. I applied for several different jobs in the workforce, but outside of a temp position at a furniture moving company, no one was willing to hire me. And this was at a time when my criminal record was pretty much clean. I can only imagine what difficulties I would face if I was to get out today. But that's another story for another day. The temp agency job was a blessing because during the time I was hired, I was literally on the verge of giving up trying to do the right thing. Yeah, I said it. I was back to trying to be a law-abiding citizen, as is my usual routine whenever I'd suffer a major failure (such as getting kicked out of school). You know, temporarily I'd strive to get back on track, and then struggle to stay there, only to eventually revert back to my old habits, which always led me right back into trouble and right back to trying to figure out how to make it right. It was a ridiculous cycle that had become my life. But with this new job, I was hoping to create a new narrative in which I maintained my good behavior for a long enough time to begin to create a new legacy, one where I'm known and loved for all the good that I do instead of being known for all the destruction I've caused.

The point I'm making is that at this point in the story, I'm at least back trying to live a 'good life', and by receiving this furniture moving gig, it appeared that my efforts were being rewarded, which was crucial for an individual like me because in order for me to stay on the right track, I needed to experience nothing but success. Because any kind of failure would send me spiraling back down the wrong path. I simply was not disciplined enough to trust the process, and I wasn't dependent upon any kind of higher power to miraculously work things out. If anything good was going to happen in my life, I was the one who was going to have to make it happen. So, once I got laid off due to a decrease in the workload acquired by the furniture company (I guess people stopped moving), and as a result was forced to stay in what you might as well call an abandoned apartment just to keep a roof over my head, I made up my mind that I was never going to go back broke. Living in that pitch black apartment surrounded by the aroma of dog feces without a dollar to my name negatively affected me in a way that is still hard for me to explain. In hindsight, the only positive thing that I think that came out of it was the confidence I developed in my ability to survive anything.

But before I continue this story, I want to send a 'shout out' to a beautiful, intelligent female codefendant of mine whom we will call 'bad news'. Without me having to ask, she came through while I was at my lowest and showed me love when I needed it most, and for that I will forever love her. Also, I must admit that there were other people to whom I could have called on or moved in with (mostly women) but moving in with one of them would have given the wrong impression and made my other females jealous. Plus, as I stated earlier, I never wanted to feel powerless in any situation, and living under someone else's roof I believe gives them too much power.

So, it was after all of this that I made the acquaintance of my co-defendant, Charlotte. We hit it off, and then eventually we moved in together. At the end of the whole sequence of us meeting and getting an apartment together, I promised his mom that I would look out for him, and as I reflect back on our time together, I remain confused about whether I fully kept that promise or not. I mean, I of course could have been a better role model by refraining from indulging in sex, drugs, and illegal activity, but for where I was in regards to my own mental and emotional stability, I protected and provided for him like he was my blood. Now would he have committed those robberies without me masterminding the whole thing? If I'm honest, I'd have to say no. Matter of fact, none of my co-defendants would have been in a position where they were forced to choose whether to roll on me for a lesser sentence or take whatever time they received from the judge or jury if it wasn't for the aggressive nature I had when it came to getting money, especially the women.

Now the guys I did crimes with, well, they were already pretty much crooks. They grew up around it and dabbled in it; the only role I played was that of a conductor to an orchestra, quarterback to a football team. That's one of the reasons I believe I was so confused about what my co-defendant, Charlotte, did during my trial. Because we all loved money and wanted more of it, we shared everything and split all proceeds down the middle. But when the 'rubber met the road' and it came time for each to account for his or her sins, I now was the only one to blame. How is that fair?. Like I said earlier, I am solely responsible for my actions, and for emboldening those around me to act negatively on their desires to obtain wealth, but at the end of the day, they were *their* desires. I'm just saying. All of the crimes that were committed by me and my 'comrades' spanned over about one and a half years; they fit into several different felony categories, but only those that I was charged with and convicted of will I openly discuss.

We were under suspicion for committing three armed robberies which led to the police snooping around our apartment complex to see if any new grand purchases had been made by us since the robberies, and also to interview our neighbors to see if they noticed any suspicious behavior on our part. It got to be so bad that I sought out a friend who had connections with a lawyer, who agreed to threaten to file a harassment/defamation suit against the police, because upon the conclusion of the interviews with our neighbors, they were told that we were bad people and advised to stay away from us.

At this point we had yet to be charged with any crime; matter of fact, to try and get ahead of the investigation, I randomly popped up at the police station when it was brought to my attention that they were going around to campus parties looking for us. Of course, when I showed up, they pretended that they were unaware of what I was referring to when I inquired about why they were looking for us. My guess was that they were unprepared, so instead of trying to scramble and fish for what little evidence they did have, they opted to send me on my way. Which didn't really bother me, because to me, that was one more day that I was able to enjoy my freedom. Because although they didn't have enough to arrest me and my co-d, they had to have something because they were absolutely barking up the right tree.

This cat and mouse game went on for about a couple of months before they finally got a subpoena to question one of my closest female friends at the time, who was also our 'get away' driver. So, they scheduled a date, brought her before the grand jury, and afterwards drove her to me and Charlotte's apartment to search the trunk of her car because it was in my possession at the time. The search turned up empty, so following it, the officers turned their attention toward me by expressing that they heard I showed up to the police station earlier to volunteer for questioning. They wondered if I'd be willing to come in again. To which I agreed because I wanted to maintain the appearance of innocence, and you couldn't convince the younger me that I wasn't smarter than the police, or anybody for that matter. So, the plan was to go in and play the victim, just another hard-working black man being falsely accused of a crime based on little or no evidence, then by the end of the interview, I would be absolved of any suspicion of guilt in their eyes. And as a result, hopefully they would then turn their attention elsewhere.

But once in the interrogation room, I may have come on a little too strongly in expressing my disdain for the corrupt judicial system, locking up men of color at much higher rates than that of whites. Going on about how they could care less whether I was innocent or not, and that their desire was to hold someone, anyone, accountable just so they could close the case. And as you can probably imagine that rhetoric really didn't go over to well with the interviewing officer, the fact that this young cocky 'nigga' had the audacity to criticize the integrity of the law and order system that they themselves had committed their lives to and did so without regard for the authority they so recklessly wield. Really pissed them off.

Which was exciting for me at the time, but was counterproductive to my mission going in, 'to absolve myself'. All I succeeded at doing was adding fuel to the fire that already burned inside of them to put me away. If they hadn't already made up their mind about finding a way to charge me with these crimes, then I know that interview pushed them over the edge, and it was because of that experience that I not too long after decided to head back to Palm Beach County. This was a decision that was extremely hard for me to make, but it was absolutely necessary if I ever wanted to get back to somewhat living a peaceful life. Because everywhere I went, it appeared that I was being followed.

CHAPTER 11

Palm Beach County

I ended up moving back into my mom and dad's, a last resort for me, because of the rules I knew they had in place from growing up there, and of course my desire as a grown adult to come and go as I pleased. I knew that there was no way that me living there was going to work, but I had to be cool and at least attempt to play nice for the time being, 'cause at that time, if I was to have been put out, then I would have been forced to shack up with one of the chicks I was dealing with. And that was a commitment I was nowhere near ready to make.

Things started off well, and were actually exceeding my expectations, until I witnessed my younger sister's husband chastise my younger brother in a way that just didn't sit well with me. And because I didn't like it, I spoke on it, and as a result, an argument ensued that led to my parents and my sister taking his side over mine. Which although it probably shouldn't have, it shocked me at the time, and it hurt me as well. To me, this dude was still an outsider and someone who couldn't be completely trusted. But I had been gone for a while, and it was now obvious that a 'changing of the guard' had taken place. I now was the outsider, and once I was made to feel that way, I began to aggressively pursue ways to get back in school. At this point, I wasn't really in the position or the mood to be picky about where it was I would go; my living conditions saw to it that the first opportunity that presented itself I more than likely would take. So, me and my pops went about the business of attempting to find or retrieve my high school highlight tape so we could send it to potential colleges in hopes that they'd give me another chance to play.

For some reason, as smart as God made me, I've always felt as if my talent on the field was all I really had to offer. I've just never thought that my mind would be the key to my success, which is something that I would say a lot of young (elite) athletes struggle with. Because from the time individuals recognize that you possess something (the 'it factor'), that most of your peers do not, then from that day on it becomes solely about maximizing your uniqueness (talent) to hopefully acquire some sort of financial gain. And whatever the exploiter or exploiters need to do to increase the likelihood of your success, they will do, even if in the long run it psychologically cripples you. One of the ways is that you're taught that your commitment to and the success of the team comes before everything, and if any other areas of your life suffer because of it, then we'll find a shortcut or two to clean it up, and most often the fix is only temporary. But that matters not, because the only thing that matters is the team.

Now, of course, all coaches and institutions are not the same. I'm sure there are many who promote the importance of obtaining a degree just as much as they promote the importance of being a committed athlete, but I unfortunately have also experienced the darker side of things, so for me not to warn you would be an unforgivable dereliction of my duty. Which is to always be honest with you about the good and bad that one may face while travelling this road called life, and at the same time absolve you of any excuse. Although there are several people out to mislead and take advantage of you, how far you go in life is completely up to you. Who you choose to listen to? And what you do with the information given you, is all up to you. Of course, there will be things that transpire throughout the course of your life that are beyond your control and may in some way negatively affect you, but how you view and respond to adversity is also completely up to you.

So, from this point in the book on, I encourage you to regain control of your life by assuming responsibility for your role in how you got to where you are in life, and then begin to change the things that you are unhappy with by doing things differently. Set short and long term goals for yourself, and schedule your day with only those activities that will help propel you in the direction of those goals. Anything outside of a little leisure time with family or friends, should strategically over time be eliminated out of your life. And the only reason I suggest strategically doing it is because I know from experience that after being engulfed in a particular lifestyle or after participating in certain activities for the majority of your life, sometimes going cold turkey can create a chaotic environment that you're not mentally and emotionally prepared to exist in. But by no means does that last statement give you license to continue to wallow in your dysfunction for as long as you can get away with it. The onus is on you to decide what poor habits can and should be stopped immediately and which ones cannot. But you can trust and believe that until you seriously go about the process of purifying your life, nothing will ever change.

While researching potential landing spots for myself, I somehow ended up in contact with one of my closest friends at the time, now my best friend, Haitian Black, who was attending the University of Dubuque in Iowa. And during this conversation we got to discussing why it was that I was now back in Florida, and what the likelihood was that I could potentially come up there. I'm sure the phone call dragged on for a while as we caught up, because when I was away at school, I had the tendency to cease communications with those back home (or also off at school). Nothing personal, I just allowed whatever scam, female, or hustle I was involved with at the time to consume my focus.

It's like the saying goes, "out of sight, out of mind", which definitely applied to me in the past, and is an area that I've grown in now, and hope to continue to grow in in the future. Because in order for me to maintain a successful marriage, I can't be out with the guys, surrounded by distractions (beautiful women), and lose sight of the fact that I have a wife. To which most may say, especially the women, "How could you forget the fact that you have a wife?" I'm not really sure because I've never officially been married, but I've had several women that I've cared for deeply, and I used to lose sight of them all the time, so I'm guessing it's the same. Even King David, a man whom God gave the title of "man after his (God's) own heart" fell victim to wandering eyes. Although there remains no excuse for it, and because men are visually motivated creatures, I believe we are more susceptible to straying from our spouse. Therefore, making it even more vital that we take certain precautions to ensure that we don't wind up in compromising situations. But that's only if we value, like we claim we do, what we've built at home.

All these platonic relationships with female friends from your past, most of which you've probably slept with, or wanted to sleep with, can potentially spell trouble if certain safeguards aren't put in place. This ranges anywhere from the topics you allow to be discussed, to how long and how often you all talk on the phone or see each other in person. You should discuss what settings are appropriate to hang out at, like should it be with a group of friends, or can you all handle it just being you two? In this case, it's important that you all are honest with yourselves and honest with each other. I know that at first glance the safeguards I suggest may seem like a lot, but if you've got a girl/woman that you love deeply and who is cool enough to allow you to have close female friends, then no measures are too extreme to protect that, I mean none.

So, my man, Haitian Black, informed me that he'd "pull up" on the head coach of their football program and inquire about whether there was still any interest in having me attend their school. I used the word "still" (even though we had never met.) because while recruiting my homeboy Haitian Black, the head coach had to have also noticed the other standouts on our team, which I was one of, and more than likely desired to recruit us as well. It was understood that we would be offered scholarships to bigger universities, and undoubtedly would choose them over Dubuque, so why bother? Which is not a backhanded diss towards my homie Haitian Black, because to be honest, out of all the elite athletes I've had the privilege to practice or play with, he is still the best one-on-one cover corner I've ever seen. Height was his only issue, or should I say the lack thereof, and other than that, I wholeheartedly believe that he would have gone to a bigger university, therefore being exposed to better coaching, and the result would have been him finding a home for himself somewhere in the league (NFL).

But due to me blowing the two previous collegiate opportunities that were presented to me, I was now praying, not literally praying, there was unfortunately still no seeking of a "higher power" at this point, that I'd get accepted into a school that earlier in the recruiting process I would have scoffed at. My how the mighty have fallen, and yet still there was no sign of me being in any way humbled by all that I had gone through, not even a little. It was as if as long as there was some way for me to manipulate or provide a way under my own strength, there was no reason to look beyond myself for any kind of guidance, spiritual or otherwise. In my mind, I was always and forever going to do me, and whatever planet, or state, I landed on/in next, it had to revolve around me. I relished in the fact that I was in complete control (at least so I thought) of my destiny. I considered myself a survivor, a problem solver, someone who, no matter what the situation, could and would find a way. Little did I know though, God was strategically positioning me to have that control taken with the force of a Mike Tyson body blow mixed with a Buster Douglas hook, a blow so powerful that it would eventually knock me to my knees, therefore forcing me into prayer position.

After a couple of days of my homeboy lobbying for me, the coach gave me a call to express his surprise in my interest in the University of Dubuque, and at the same time, his delight that I desired to come there. My response was one of gratitude and excitement, excited over the change of scenery, of course, but grateful about the fact that I had been granted yet another opportunity to try and get my life right. Not in any spiritual sense, but by getting my life right I meant do better as far as the decisions I had been making. Like simply going to class when I was supposed to, slowing down on the sex, drugs, and the chasing of money. Correction, the illegal chasing of the money, cause we all know that money is the one thing you can't operate in this world without.

During the convo with the coach, he asked me whether I wanted to come in the spring, which was about a month or so away, or wait for the fall semester to come around. Based on how my current living arrangement (with my parents) was going, what do you think I said? You're absolutely correct if you guessed that I opted to take part in the spring semester as opposed to waiting for the fall. Simply put, I was on the first thing smoking to a place I knew absolutely nothing about. But I ended up having the time of my life while there. So, with my financial aid situation in order and flight booked, I was on my way to yet another "fun house" in hopes that the outcome of this trip would be far different from that of the others. I mean they do say that the "third times a charm", right?

CHAPTER 12

Dubuque

For the most part, my time there was charmed, I refrained from all illegal activity in order to obtain financial gain, outside of one incident when I took a trip back to Virginia to visit a friend and ended pulling a *lick*. But as far as my stay in Iowa was concerned, me robbing people at gunpoint was a thing of the past. I was trying to get as far away from the chaos I had created in Virginia as possible, so that meant retiring from any and all illegal activity. I wanted no unnecessary heat drawn to me that might reignite the passion that I thought had died out for my conviction of the robberies I was suspected of. So, I worked hard to transform myself into a student athlete. I went to class regularly, I worked out and practiced the way a committed athlete would, and, for the most part, even obeyed the rules of the dormitory where I was a resident.

We had one minor issue where someone accidentally left my dorm room door open at the same time that the campus security was doing their rounds, and it was discovered that I had a refrigerator full of liquor. As this was a clear violation of the housing rules, they had to express their disdain for me having violated the ordinances by confiscating and pouring the liquor out right in front of me. I honestly have never been so disgusted with the waste of anything until that day. In fact, I was so disturbed by it that I went right back to the liquor store to purchase another bottle to mourn the loss of the others. I had to let them (the wasted bottles) know that they were missed, and that they were not sacrificed in vain.

But all jokes aside, that cop taking over a hundred dollars' worth of alcohol from me really would've pissed me off had I not been flooded with money from that *lick* I told you about (or didn't tell you about). Around that time, I was really partying hard, but for the first time I was doing so in moderation (choosing to wait until the weekends). I guess I had morphed into what one might call a *functional* party animal, while still somehow being able to fulfill the expectations that came along with being a college athlete.

I met a lot of interesting women while there and had several more that were still a part of my life from the short time that I spent in Virginia, so that made it a lot easier for me to resist the temptation to indulge in any kind of criminal activity. They were extremely supportive of me and were always there when I needed them. So much so, that my lady friend allowed me to put her in direct contact with my landlord at the time, so she could transfer the cost of my rent directly to him without me having to play the middleman. It was sent every month on time, which enabled me to focus solely on school and playing ball. She was an incredible woman, one whom I took for granted, and definitely should have been more honest with about where she fit in my 'master plan' (assuming I had one). Instead, I allowed her to believe that there could possibly be a scenario where we could wind up together, not that I was specifically promising these things, but when you know that a woman (or man) has deep feelings for you and you play on that (those feelings) instead of clearly specifying where you stand in regards to your feelings, then you are kinda promising without promising, or giving false hope.

As for the guys I linked up with while in Iowa, *supportive* is not the word that I would use. They were cool, but not particularly the type to encourage you to do anything constructive with your life. While with them, my focus was pretty much on how we could have a good time, and our idea of having a good time was drinking, getting high, and sleeping with as many women as we could get our hands on. Which if you aren't guided by any kind of moral compass and have no dreams or aspirations to do anything greater, then spending the majority of your free time engaging in these activities is considered acceptable. But if you want more for your life (like I was beginning to want at that point.), then these pastimes are undoubtedly a waste of time, and if done too often, will eventually derail you. And this is not a backhanded attempt to criticize the character of the individuals I ran with, or me blaming them for the mistakes that I made. I am solely responsible for the decisions I made from the day I first met them up until my incarceration.

But I bring them up (and the time we spent together) to emphasize the point that while I was interacting with them, it wasn't yet clear to me that in order for me to continue to progressively move away from the overindulgence of these activities (drinking, smoking, and chasing women), it was necessary for me to change the type of company I kept. There's a quote that says, "Show me your friends, and I'll show you your future." Still in my early twenties at the time, I was naive to the truth attached to such a quote, and therefore ended up learning the hard way. At one time or another all of us wound up incarcerated, me having acquired the most time of us all. So, while speaking to the influence they may have had on me, I must also admit that I could have been a better role model myself. Because although they were their own men, looking back, I always have possessed more power and influence then I would have liked to admit.

My mom used to constantly tell me that I was a leader of those that were around me. Not wanting the responsibility that comes along with leading a group of individuals, I would always shy away from it by either simply denying it or stating that I didn't want to be anybody's 'leader'. But some roles in life you just kind of wind up in, and life doesn't care how you feel about it. Prime example: my older sister whining about being the 'foster parent' to my brother's kids after she had raised her own daughter to adulthood and was finally getting used to the idea of being able to finally focus on herself. Yet in spite of all the time and energy she had already dedicated to her family and career (teacher), when it was finally her time to relax and simply enjoy the fruits of her labor, she was thrust right back into a leadership position she thought she had experienced the last of. So, like her, being a leader was never really optional for me because even though she could have turned a blind eye and allowed the foster system to take the kids, that's not how our family operates, so there was no other choice.

Based on the stature and personality that God gave me, no matter where I am or who I come into contact with, I will always eventually become one of the leading voices in the room. Which at one point would have been a terrifying thought for me but based on the fact that I now know that God is with me, and has called me to lead, I strive to embrace leadership opportunities. Of course, there were steps that I had to take in order to get to this point (a leader of men), a spiritual journey that I'm still on that had to be embarked on, and a series of tests that I had to take. It has been a roller coaster ride as I've walked with Christ, with seasons of my life appearing that I'm on a permanent trajectory to the top, and seasons when it feels like the downward spiral won't ever stop. Yet when I reflect on what my life has been like apart from Christ, and the joy I've experienced even during the low moments since being adopted by Christ, I would much rather be a recipient of His amazing grace then trying to live life my own way.

Which brings me to my favorite part of the book, where you now get to discover how I got to know Christ, and why ten years later and counting, he is still the Lord of my life. Please continue to walk with me.

CHAPTER 13

Wake Up Call

Well, like I've mentioned previously, I was born into a Christian household but never really had a desire to know Christ. I went to church with my mother while growing up, and even participated in a few Bible studies with my pops while at home, because he rarely went to any church that wasn't run by him. I often used to think that if he had taken more of a leadership role in regard to our family's faith, then maybe I would have showed more interest. But honestly, if me watching him attempt to start his own church in our home, and me taking part in the Bible studies he ran wasn't enough, then nothing he did would have worked. It was just my lot in life to play the role of the prodigal son, to venture out on my own to learn the tough lessons that life has a way of teaching you when you don't live it the right way. And as you can see, that's exactly what I did. I chose to live life the way that I saw fit, as opposed to the way that I was consistently and correctly instructed to when I was younger, therefore leading me to one of two destinations, a lengthy prison sentence or an early death.

Thankfully, so far, I've been spared from the latter, and I wholeheartedly believe that it's because God so graciously saw fit to allow the former. Yes, you heard me correctly; I believe prison saved my life, literally and figuratively. Literally because, although while in Iowa, I was trending in the right direction, if things had ever gotten so bad that I was on the verge of losing everything, then there is no doubt that I would have picked up the pistol again and possibly been killed in the commission of a robbery, either by the victim or police. And figuratively because I was spiritually dead, lost in sin, and if I had died in that state, I would have gone to hell for eternity. And why am I so convinced of this, you ask?

Well, it's simple. I've had several so called 'wakeup-calls' prior to my prison stint, but it wasn't until I got charged in Iowa and was potentially facing thirty years that I finally took a long hard look at the direction of my life, and the individuals I'd allowed in it. And as a result, I began to spend more and more time home alone. I mean for the first time in a long time, I could actually hear myself think, during which God the Father began gently nudging me in the direction of a nearby church. A church that as much as I had passed it, I paid zero attention to it. But God being who He is, and knowing exactly what I needed, spoke to me in a voice that spookily seemed audible, revealed to me His existence, and told me I needed to go there, so I went. I'm not sure what day I heard the audible voice, but that very next Sunday I entered Kingdom Ministries with really no idea what to expect and no intentions on participating in any way.

Once inside I instantly felt comfortable and experienced a sense of peace that I had never felt before which caused me to engage in the praise and worship service and introduce myself to those that readily made themselves available. Normally I'm not so friendly. Looking back on it now, it reminded me a lot of my grandmother's church in Sanford, Florida (just a little bigger), so that is probably what led to the high level of comfortability I felt. Probably. But whatever it was, and for whatever it's worth, I left the service feeling great and had made up my mind that I was going back the next week, which was a major step for me, because a long time ago I had made up in my mind that I would never step foot into a church again until I was completely ready to surrender my life to Christ. And at that moment, although I felt good, I didn't feel that. I just knew that in the presence of the Lord was where I needed to be at least once a week, and maybe that would help wash away some of the fornicating I was doing Monday through Sunday. Yes, Sunday too, and sometimes not long after church, but bear in mind that I was still not yet saved, and as soon as I decided that I was going to start attending church, it seemed as if the temptation ramped up tenfold. The enemy definitely didn't want me to apply anything the minister spoke about to my life. So, whenever I wasn't inside the church, he did his best to keep me distracted. At the same time, God was steadily drawing me closer and closer to Him, and because of that, my determination never wavered as far as honoring my commitment to show up to church that very next week goes.

Meanwhile, the spirit and the flesh were warring for dominion in my life, yet I was still doing my best to keep my nose clean by attending school and checking in once a week to my pretrial probation officer. All while preparing to fight the charges I had pending. At this point, my situation was still in the early stages of the court proceedings, so I figured it would be a while before any decision was made, and the one bright spot that I had going for me was that my criminal history was minimal. So, I came to reason that if I was able to postpone my court dates until I finished summer school, I would have enough positive, with a healthy recommendation from my P.O. (probation officer), ammunition to present to the judge to hopefully get off with a couple years' probation, and therefore be able to finish obtaining my degree. Whether my plan would work or not was yet to be seen, but as promised though, I kept secretly going to church, because no one close to me knew about it, hoping for nothing more than a 'quick fix' (that spiritual high you get from a good sermon) like I had gotten the first time I went.

As I hoped, every time was just as good as the first. But on the third Sunday, the Lord moved on my heart in such a way that I fell to my knees in tears at the altar mumbling something about not wanting to live like this any longer. I had finally reached the point of exhaustion when it came to me ripping and running the streets. I just wanted to be free from the lifestyle that for so long had imprisoned me; I was a slave to everything that was unholy, and while living that type of lifestyle temporarily satisfied/numbed the pain, it inevitably led me deeper into despair. So, at the altar, eyes blurred by tears, and heartbroken, I surrendered what was left of my life in hopes that God could mold me like a patch of flimsy clay into something worthy of being saved. I left the church that day no longer feeling ashamed of the life I had lived, or the man I had become. I felt redeemed, and like when God renamed Jacob to Israel, God had also given me a new identity. One that if lived out to its fullest potential would lead to me leaving a lasting legacy that me, my family, and offspring could/would be proud of. One where He is the Lord of my life, and therefore will be glorified throughout my growth process all the way up until it's completion, which won't take place until I finally reach heaven.

Until then though, a process is just what it is; it doesn't all happen overnight, which is what most people have a hard time grasping. Initially some habits God may grace you to rid yourself of immediately, but most of which you're dealing with, He will gradually deliver you from to strengthen your appreciation for Him and how far He has brought you.

Your testimony is also strengthened/developed throughout this time, meaning that when the time comes for you to share it, you'll possess a higher level of confidence because you've grown to know God in a much deeper way. A way that only can come through having to lean on God while in the eye of the storm. Similar to when Christ waited for Lazarus to be put in the tomb before He showed up, the outcome of your situation will leave no doubt that there is a God and that He rules and reigns in your life..

It's also important for us to be patient. Patient with the process, and patient with those that are going through it. Because us not being patient with ourselves can open the door for the enemy to drown us in self-condemnation. And not being patient with others can lead to them feeling overwhelmed with pressure to please or put on a facade for those that didn't die for their souls, and potentially lose sight of the one who did. I know from firsthand experience that an individual like myself can go from giving my life to Christ one Sunday, to skipping church the next time to sinfully dive between some cheeks, and still have a sincere desire to honor God. Which is exactly what went on in the early going of me striving to develop an intimate relationship with Christ.

I fell short quite often, so much so, that it appeared that as long as I was surrounded by all these women (distractions) there was no way I was going to be able to take hold of the abundant life for which I had been redeemed. At that time, lust had way too strong of a hold on me, but once again, Christ being who He is, and being committed to my success, allowed the state of Virginia to issue me an out-of-state warrant that caused my bond to be revoked. Which forced Iowa to re-incarcerate me, snatched me from the 'teeth of the beast' (the streets), and thankfully put me in a place where I'd be apart from all of the hindrances I faced.

Once back in jail, my court proceedings moved a lot more quickly due to the fact that there was no longer any reason to buy more time because upon the completion of my Iowa case, I now had Virginia to contend with, a place I dreaded going, because even though I was unaware of how severe my situation was there, I had a strong feeling inside that I was in a whole lot of trouble, and that if they had found enough evidence to indict me, then it was evident that someone had sold their soul by agreeing to serve me up on a platter. I wasn't really too concerned about Iowa though; I had a good lawyer who fought as hard as she could to get me a reasonable plea based on my minimal criminal history and the likelihood of whether I could beat the charge had I gone all the way (to trial), plus they had parole. She did an incredible job, and I thank God for her patience with me throughout the process because we had some heated discussions whenever she brought me a plea that I deemed unsatisfactory. Yet still she worked with me, and fought for me, until we got the prosecution to run my 5-year and 10-year sentence concurrent, leaving me with a 10-year plea agreement that the judge had to sign off on.

⬦

CHAPTER 14

Spiritual Battles

My time in Dubuque county jail went pretty smooth. I was in constant communication with my family and the select few women I allowed to remain in my corner at that time. My cell partners were all pretty cool, and I was able to share the gospel with most of them. But there was one that was as powerful as he was faith wise, my experience while living with him was a wild one to say the least. Him we'll call Mustard Seed, because he wholeheartedly believed that his faith could move mountains, walls, and whatever else that stood in his way. And me being so young in the faith (Christianity), I argued with him constantly about his faith being strong enough to do the things he professed it could, but he never wavered in his convictions. And that was incredible for me to see so early on in my spiritual journey because that was the same level of resolve that I was going to have to develop if I was to survive two criminal proceedings in two different states, actually do the time I would be sentenced to do and get out with my faith still intact. Faith aside though, Mustard Seed was extremely intelligent, and a bit crazy, which I think you have to be in order to develop faith like his, or at least you'll look that way to the world.

Mustard Seed had a woman that he was crazy about, and that drove him crazy as well because she had a tendency to fool around, a fact he knew about her before they entered into the relationship, but that's a different story for a different day. And as a result of the stress caused by his wife's infidelity, and the fact that I know that the enemy didn't want him to continue to 'walk by faith' (and motivate others to do so as well, like he had done me), he used to have what I thought were nightmares. It turns out that he was being tormented in his sleep by a demonic spirit. Like I said though, at first I didn't know what to think. I used to hear him moaning throughout the night and feel the vibrations of the bunk beds as he tossed and turned. I'm talking he tossed so violently that it was impossible for me to sleep. At the end of the day, sleep was the last thing on my mind. As you can probably imagine this was a bit frightening for a 23 year old who has never spent more than a week behind bars, so having no prior experience to draw from, I simply got up and stood with my back to the wall and waited for what I thought was his nightmare to stop. Once it did, I would find my way back to my bunk and attempt to get some rest, which in spite of the attacks, most nights I would have no problem doing.

But one night, after I went to lay back down once his episode appeared to be over, I was attacked by this invisible dark force that had me pinned to my bed and felt like it was attempting to enter me. I had never felt a force so powerful and so relentless as this, one that caught me completely off guard, and that I had no knowledge of how to defeat. Keep in mind that I was only about three months removed from when I first surrendered my life to Christ, so angels and demons are things that I of course have heard of, but at the same time am still struggling to believe in, let alone know how to deal with one if I so happened to have an encounter with one. So, at that moment I was like a samurai without a sword, or a preacher without a sermon. At least so I thought.

But God quickly showed me that when I have no strength left to fight, or insight to develop a strategy to fight with, all that is left is all that I need, and that is to call on his Holy Majestic name. Which, in a moment of panic, is exactly what I decided to do. I uttered the name of Jesus in all of His glory repeatedly until the evil spirit loosed its grip on me, and had I not, I'm sure that it would have took complete hold of me, probably to the point where I would have been roaming the cell naked like the demon possessed man in the Bible who roamed the tombs, and was a danger not only to himself, but to others as well. Well maybe that's a bit extreme, because that man in the Bible was consumed by a legion (meaning many) of demons, whereas I thankfully only had to tussle with one. But judging by what my cell partner was going through, it's safe to say that it definitely wouldn't have been an enjoyable time had the name of Jesus not caused it to flee.

To be honest, I had a difficult enough time staying on the straight and narrow without the added influence of a demonic spirit. But the start to my faith walk was strong, so much so, that an officer at Dubuque county jail who had the opportunity to watch and get to know me, expressed on the day that I was set to be transported to the Iowa prison receiving center that, "You didn't deserve to be locked up."

He said that he had seen a lot of inmates come and go during his time as an officer that *did* belong in prison, but that I was not one of them.

At the time though, the significance of that statement didn't really hit me, as was natural for me, the first thought I received upon hearing him say that was, "You should have seen me prior to surrendering my life to Christ."

If he had met me just a few months sooner, he absolutely would have been singing a different tune. But he hadn't, and in spite of how factual that thought may have been, that individual who I so readily identified with was no longer who I was.

Yet I had a difficult time seeing myself any other way. It wasn't until years later that I began to become somewhat more comfortable with accepting compliments from people in reference to my character, and I say 'somewhat' because I still sometimes struggle with it today. I'm sure many people do struggle, people who have sought to reform their lives, especially after being referred to with so many negative terms for majority of your life. Being called a troublemaker, stupid, dumb, slut, or "you'll never amount to anything", can influence how you view yourself, and as a result make it extremely difficult to see yourself any other way regardless of how much you've changed.

Periodically throughout this journey called life I was referred to as being many things that are not considered positive in the English language, and the strange thing is that I don't believe that those who chose to label me such things even meant any harm. They were simply describing the behavior that I was exhibiting at that time. I say that because most who speak derogatory towards you normally do so to harm you, or to sabotage your growth, but in my case, I was surrounded by people who simply saw me for who I was at the time and chose to speak on it. It could have been that they cared enough to say, "Mike, you jive trippin."

God using them to reveal to me how off course I had gotten by shining a light on my questionable behavior. Whatever it was, it stuck with me for quite some time until I was able to learn to fully receive the love that God gives. Finally realizing that God's love remains consistent even when I error at times was the key to me learning to love myself, and to me embracing the compliments expressed by the outside world for being the 'light' that I was created to be.

The trip to the Iowa receiving center was a short one, as was my stay. I believe that I was only there a good thirty days before the state of Virginia came to retrieve me so I might be held accountable for my sins there. The only thing that really stands out to me about the receiving center was that it was coed, so we got to see the female inmates every now and then. We shared the same medical intake center.

An officer asked me, "Have you ever been here before?"

Which I believe he felt compelled to ask based on how comfortable I appeared in my surroundings, which has never really been the case, but when you operate without fear dictating your actions then it will come off as if you're at ease, or at peace with what's going on. To be honest, peace with the outcome of my court proceedings and being incarcerated didn't come for a while, and even when it did finally come, I wavered in it, and still do. There was never a time in my bid that I wasn't praying to/pleading with God trying to get home.

CHAPTER 15

Back to VA

So, Virginia came and got me, basically paraded me through a crowded airport, put me on a commercial plane, and we were on our way. The U.S. marshals that were in charge of my transport were extremely cool, and although the circumstances surrounding the trip sucked, it was rather enjoyable. The marshals were professional in their approach to the transport to ensure my safety and also the safety of others. And I think that's worth mentioning because while being incarcerated (as I'm sure most inmates could attest to) there have been several times when I've been treated as or made to feel like less than a human being, surrounded by officers who get a kick out of striving to humiliate you. Yet these guys didn't take that approach, and for that I think that they should be applauded. It's police like them that actually give you hope that once the racist and 'trigger happy thrill seekers' are eliminated, we possibly can create a system where the people and law enforcement can work together.

Upon arriving at the Virginia airport, the officers had a car waiting, and after a quick bite to eat, I was delivered to the Rockingham County Jail, where I was processed and held in booking until they were able to find me a cell. By the time they were finally through sending officer after officer to offer me immunity to help them close a couple of the cases that they suspected I had done, my body was screaming for a cell. Why? Because in booking, there was no pillow or mattress to sleep on, and on top of that, it was freezing cold, which is probably why they kept me there so long, hoping that extreme discomfort would force me into cooperating. But when they finally did get me to the pod that I would be staying in, it turned out that it was the best possible place for me. You could tell right from the jump that God was ordering my steps and had a plan for me being there. That's not to say that I didn't experience any turbulence along the way, but when reflected on in its totality, it was undeniably evident that my time there was physically and spiritually beneficial not only for me, but also for those who surrounded me. Physically because that's where I first decided to fully dedicate myself to being more health conscious, by working out and somewhat monitoring what I ate. And spiritually because it's often in the darkest and most difficult of times that you are forced to learn to trust God the most, and there were also several instances where I was able to be used by God to pray with and encourage those around me.

Instantly I experienced the favor of God, and before I even really got settled, I unexpectedly was anointed as the spiritual leader over those men, a role I had never played before, but felt like it came quite natural to me. Shortly after my arrival, I remember a Hispanic dude coming to my cell because his daughter, who had not long just been born, was now back in the hospital in need of some type of surgery and he desired to pray. So, pray is what we locked hands and did, and as is the norm with the mighty God that I serve, he showed up and saw to it that the young man's daughter's surgery went well, and she wound up recovering rather quickly. I also remember initially working out by myself, but not too long after I had started, the whole pod joined me in a few of the workouts, I mean literally the whole pod. Doing everything from pushups to squats, jogging to pull-ups, all under my direction as their trainer. It was a role that I was unfamiliar with at that time, but while fulfilling it, I felt an extreme sense of purpose and an abundance of joy. Like I said earlier in regard to being anointed as the spiritual leader, I also felt that physical training came quite naturally to me. I mean already having the personality of one who draws and gets along with all types of people, once the crowd has been gathered, I then simply had only to draw from the wealth of knowledge I had acquired from the college courses I took and from the years I spent working out during my athletic career. The positive impact that I was having on the pod was undeniable.

All of this was going on while I was struggling to make peace with the things that I had. Which speaks to the grace that God had bestowed upon me to help me to thrive in spite of the storm, the storm being that one of the people I had grown to love and trust the most had turned their back on me by testifying against me to acquire a lesser sentence. This was something that infuriated me in a way that few other circumstances had, and something that if I was serious about becoming who God created me to be, that I was going to have to forgive and move on from. As you can probably guess, this was easier said than done, because I loved this individual like he was my blood and would have died for him like he was my brother, so when he betrayed me, it hurt me to my core. All kinds of vengeful thoughts crossed my mind as I would reflect on what he had done, thoughts that I care not to elaborate on because even now it would put me in a negative space. This is ten years after I had come to grips with the fact that had I not done what I'd done, then there wouldn't have been anything to tell.

So ultimately, it's my fault that I wound up in the predicament that I had found myself in, and Lord knows that I'm cool with that. Regardless of the clear understanding that I have of the whole situation and the faith I have in Christ, there will forever be rules (street rules) that I believe should never be broken under any circumstances. And to do so, in my mind, makes you a coward. Therefore, this is someone I will never respect. It's bad enough because of my faith I gotta let him live, but my respect I cannot give.

But God graced me to thrive anyhow, and I found it very therapeutic to write and read during my alone time. As a result, I discovered an artist gene that enabled me to create poetry. Day after day God showed me how to use the negative energy, aka that which the devil meant for harm, to create something beautiful that helped me and could potentially help others to grow from the trauma they incur. It was also during this time, in the midst of one of my intense prayer sessions where I was struggling to hear the voice of the Lord and see him at work in my circumstance, that He revealed to me the seriousness of what I had done and how I deserved to be disciplined for that reason. But at the same time, I felt His reassuring presence that silently said to me that in spite of the chaos I had caused, He would be there with me every step of the way, and even deliver me once He prepared me and a place for me to rule and reign. So, upon the completion of that particular prayer session, I felt that it was God's will for me to plead guilty, therefore assuming complete responsibility for what I had done, leaving the time that I would be sentenced to in the hands of the judge (technically), but ultimately in the hands of God.

I revealed this revelation to my lawyer, who then proceeded to try to talk me out of it, but I was so strong in my conviction that this was the path that Christ would have me take that, although he didn't agree, he stopped fighting me. What his motives were behind him trying to talk me out of it I may never know, but throughout the course of our private meetings together, he brought the ideas of me 'playing crazy' (pretending to be insane) and/or following my codefendants example of rolling on (snitching) anyone I could think of. My response was that during the commission of these crimes I was fully aware of what I was doing, and to the latter idea, that I didn't care if they sentenced me to life in prison, I would never cooperate with the state by way of snitching on someone else. And if he disrespected me again by bringing it up, he would be immediately replaced. He also attempted to get Mom involved in persuading me to 'rat' and I told her the same thing, which was that if she desired to continue to be a consistent part of my life, then she need not ever come at me like that again. On the day she does, it will be the last time that we would ever speak.

I know a lot of you are probably thinking, *Would he really cut off the woman that brought him into this world?* And the answer to that is, absolutely and unequivocally, hell yea. I'm extremely stubborn when it comes to the principles that I strive daily to build my life upon. When it comes to staying true to who I am, and standing firm on what I believe, there ain't no wavering in me. Fortunately, we never revisited the subject, so things never had to go that far, and thankfully because my mom has proved to be a great spiritual advisor, and an even better friend, one whom I'd hate to have to replace. There were several times that while fighting my case in Virginia, that my faith began to dwindle, and she listened to me vent about how God never seemed to really be there when I needed Him the most. She encouraged me in those times, prayed for and with me often, even once keeping me from beating up a dude that was the guiding force in having basically the entire pod turn on me.

<>

CHAPTER 16

Windstorm

This particular incident took place about a month or so in, and on the day of the incident that led to the falling out, I so happened to be in the day room of the pod when a group of inmates decided that it was a good idea to pretend as if they were going to rape this older white guy, who was clearly uncomfortable with what was going on yet was too afraid to speak up. So, as I witnessed what was going on and recognized the discomfort that this inmate was experiencing, I felt the spirit of the Lord encouraging me to speak on his behalf, so speak I did. And as a result, one dude who was the instigator of them picking on the older guy felt "some type of way", I'm sure it was probably because he had never been checked prior to this experience in regards to his behavior. Regardless of why it was, he was clearly out of line (along with everyone else who participated) and needed to be straightened.

The response to my chastisement was, "If he has a problem with the treatment he's experiencing, then he would say so."

I told him, "It's obvious he isn't into being played with like that! He hasn't said anything because he's scared to."

It baffled me at the time that they seemed so oblivious to how their actions were affecting this individual, but before it was time for me to leave this jail (Rockingham County Jail), I would be forced to see how my actions negatively impacted the victims of my crimes, therefore enabling me to understand. How my own 'self-awakening' moment came about we will discuss a little later on, but for now there's more to the story behind me being at odds with the residents of the pod I was in.

Once the back and forth was finished between me and those who tried to justify their behavior, we all kind of went to our own separate quarters, which wasn't difficult to do because our pod was a max pod, housing only violent offenders. We all had a single man cell. I loved this for many reasons as you could probably imagine, the major one being the alone time to read and pray. Having a cell to myself while enduring the mental and spiritual pressure that was being applied from all sides while there in Virginia was a Godsend, and helped my spiritual growth take an enormous leap in the right direction. I slept well that night, woke up the next morning feeling refreshed, and was unaware of the backlash that was to come from me speaking up for the victim of the pod harassment. The thought of that situation carrying over to the next day never even crossed my mind, especially since during the confrontation, no insults were thrown, nor any subliminal disses that could lead to one party or the other feeling disrespected to the point of feeling the need to disassociate oneself from the other or come to blows. But then again, I was still fairly new to the pod, and the knowledge I had of who these individuals that I was locked up with actually was limited. The fact that the situation did spill over into the next day was evidence that those with whom I was dealing with were not on the same maturity level that I was.

So, once they woke up and we all finally wound up in the day room together, there was a noticeable tension in the pod that put me on edge and led to me feeling that I might need to get the jump on one of them if I was to have any kind of a chance to get out of this situation in one piece. Naturally, once again being thrust into a hostile environment, my survival instincts kicked in, and almost caused me to potentially put myself in a situation where I might have to take someone's life. That may sound a bit extreme to those on the outside, but in prison the slightest 'windstorm' can turn into a 'hurricane', and if you can't or are unwilling to match the other person's wind speed then there's a great chance you're going to get blown away. So, going in, you have to be prepared to go as hard and as long as it takes to ensure that your life isn't the one that's taken, even if that means taking the life of someone else. It's a sad reality, but it's reality still, so you do what you can to avoid putting yourself in situations like that. But when an issue does come your way, then as a man, you stand. In my case, standing wasn't enough. I was ready to initiate the physical altercation between me and those in the pod that may have thought they wanted war with me, because in my mind, based on past experiences, it would be foolish of me to sit around and wait for them to dictate the rules of engagement.

Since I was an adolescent, I've always been taught to strike first, and never to stop until your opponent has been defeated. And it's thanks to that strategy that I've been fortunate enough to have been on the winning side of the majority of my fights. So how does the saying go? "If it ain't broke, then don't fix it." And if my past experiences have taught me anything, it's that when you're forced to face any kind of adversity, the likelihood of your success is far greater when you go for what you know, as opposed to experimenting with a technique that is unproven. Thankfully, my mom and I remained in contact with each other because she was available whenever I needed someone to talk to, and/or talk me down (aka talk me out of doing something crazy), and it was her words of wisdom working in tandem with the Holy Spirit that kept me at bay. Day after day for about a series of two weeks I would maintain basically the same routine in the attempt to remain focused and not be drawn out by the threatening looks of a few who sought to intimidate me.

That routine consisted of my daily prayer and study time, a 40 minute or so workout, then in the afternoon, once I'd showered and was in the mood for a fun-filled distraction, I would play gin rummy with the only person who hadn't shunned me, a Hispanic guy from El Salvador. Due to his limited English, he was oblivious to what was going on, yet we had a ball every night that we played. Of course, as is the pattern with me, I didn't really realize the significance of the role that he played in my life at that time, but in hindsight I see how God used him to help increase the joy I experienced while in my 'war room' by being someone that at the end of the day I could laugh with while enjoying a fun filled game. I really needed that during those couple of weeks, and God being as faithful and loving as He is, saw fit to smile down on me by way of sending an angel from El Salvador.

Fast forwarding a bit (because that routine and me being at odds with these guys lasted a few weeks), one day when I was praying and meditating on that which I had read for that particular day, I heard the word of the Lord clear as day say, "Go talk to them."

My reply was, "Go talk to who"?

Even though I knew who it was He meant, but like when God commanded Jonah to go and preach to the people of Nineveh, I definitely was not trying to humble myself to that extent. So, allowing my flesh to have its way for a bit, I tried to ignore and pass it off as if it wasn't the

Holy Spirit, when I clearly knew that it was. The problem was that, even though it resonated in my spirit, it didn't make sense to my mind, which spiritual things rarely make sense when viewed from an earthly perspective. So, I shook it off and went back to attempting to meditate on what it was I thought God really wanted me to focus on, His Word. But it turned out that what God wanted was me to humble myself by putting his Word into action. And He made that completely clear by reiterating to me twice that which He told me to do earlier, basically leaving me with no excuse, and zero doubt that this was His will. Therefore, I was left with two choices, to either be obedient and trust God to guide me or allow my pride to potentially destroy for me the opportunity to be used by God in this situation by exhibiting Christlike conflict resolution. I was reminded during this time that I said that if I ever got around to giving my life to Christ that I would "serve him with all that I had", and if there's anything that I pride myself on, it's being a man of my word.

So, in spite of the confusion I experienced concerning why it was He wanted me to go talk to these individuals (because me talking to them was why I was technically in this mess), and how uncomfortable it made me, I put on what would be considered my workout/fighting apparel and proceeded to go downstairs where they were stationed at the time. Once down there, I saw the leader of the 'rebellion' and the Hispanic gangbanger whom I had prayed with only weeks earlier for the health of his daughter sitting in his cell.

I approached the cell, asked them could I speak with them, and with the Hispanic guy's approval, I entered. I could instantly tell by the body language of the leader that he wasn't interested in hearing anything I had to say, yet as opposed to allowing it to discourage my efforts to seek peace, I chose to stay the course and at least attempt to talk it out the way God had commanded me.

I explained, "As a man, I stand behind everything I said that night. If in your eyes I said or done something to offend you, then I apologize because that wasn't my intent."

The Hispanic guy embraced the spirit of the meeting; the leader did not.

Upon me finishing what it was I had to say, and the Hispanic guy giving me the head nod (as if to say that we were cool), the leader stormed out of the room, lightly brushing against me on the way out, which caused me to lose every ounce of civility that I had left in me.

I immediately turned around and responded by saying, "Why would you walk off while I'm trying to talk to you?"

He said something along the lines of, "I ain't trynna hear that."

Which further infuriated me, and I came back with, "Since you don't want to work this out peacefully, then you know where my cell is."

This was of course insinuating that we could *rumble* (fight) whenever he wanted to, which was absolutely the wrong way to go about handling his reaction. But the fact is that even though I chose to walk in obedience by going to talk to them in the first place, and I knew I was doing the right thing, I still felt a bit weak for doing so. This wasn't normally how I handled situations such as this, it was hard enough for me to ignore the hateful looks I was being given and not take matters into my own hands. But on top of me humbling myself by allowing God to avenge the unjust treatment against me, God asked me to prostrate myself even more by reaching out to these guys (which I had no intention of doing, because I was fine with it just being me and God), and when I did, this dude chose to take it as an opportunity to 'carry me" like I was some kind of chump, and I wasn't feeling that.

So, at that point, I had said what I said, and it was what it was. But he never took me up on my offer, so things pretty much continued in the fashion that they had prior to the talk. He obviously being consumed by his hatred for me, and me striving to improve my level of integrity by reading, writing, praying, and doing whatever else the spirit of the Lord would have for me to do. I have to ask that you forgive me though, because I'm not completely sure how long after the 'talk' it was until the Lord resolved this situation. But as to move on and not become fixated on the accuracy of the time, we'll say it was a few weeks.

I woke up early one morning, as is my usual routine, to retrieve my breakfast tray, and then went back to my cell to enjoy the meal that had been provided for me. From the way the day started, it appeared that it would be just like any other day. Just moments after finishing my meal, I heard a commotion downstairs that caused me to rise to my feet and go see what was happening. Once downstairs, I came to find that the leader was at odds with a white dude in the pod that from my limited time there seemed not to bother anyone. In spite of that, he found himself in a physical altercation with the leader."

Dude had a knack for picking on what he thought were defenseless white boys, but I guess he finally barked up the wrong tree because this particular white boy was far from helpless. And proved as much once the verbal altercation became physical. Though he started out slow, based on him having more endurance than the leader, he eventually got the better of him. The police then came after what felt like them fighting for about half an hour, which is not unusual in jail or the penitentiary due to most prisons being understaffed and overpopulated. I've seen people get beaten mercilessly for an excessive amount of time and the authorities not even be aware of what went on until days later. And that's if they find out at all because most assaults go unreported. Behind these walls you can actually get yourself in even more trouble by involving the police in your business because then you'll be identified as a snitch wherever you go, a label that there is no way back from, and that will compel some inmates to make your life a living hell strictly for kicks.

But getting back to the story. Once the police broke up the fight, they commanded all those who weren't involved to report to their cells while they sorted things out, so I did just that. And probably about ten minutes later, I sensed a presence at the door of my cell which caused me to put my prayer on hold and look to see who it was. As ridiculous as it might sound, it was the leader. Why he was at my door was initially a mystery to me, but once I looked up, he made it completely clear that he wasn't feeling me. Which I already knew, and I felt the same way about him, but the major difference was that now I was locked behind a cell door and couldn't respond physically to his remarks. How convenient for him to all of a sudden get some balls and confront me about what I said weeks prior about him and his homeboys picking on an old white dude, especially when I had already invited him to my cell, and he opted not to come.

I'll let you discern actually how eager you think he was to do what he was now expressing that he wanted to do, which was to put his hands on me. But in spite of the little stunt he pulled, I responded with not a word. I knew he was fronting, plus I've never been the type to participate in frivolous trash talking with anyone in an attempt to prove that my nuts hang further then the next man's. He and I both knew what time it was, which is why he handled it like he did, but because of the scene he made, an officer came to my door to see who he was talking to, and then took it upon himself to put me and him on a keep away list. This prevented us from ever crossing paths again as long as we were both in that particular jail together, which didn't bother me none, because I had no desire to see him again, nor did I have any desire to seek revenge against him.

Did I like him? Absolutely not. Did I enjoy seeing the white boy he fought get the ups on him? I sure did. But at the end of the day, I had committed myself to honoring God in this situation, so as long as he had refrained from the appearance of seriously wanting to harm me, then I had to maintain my composure as well. I bring up those two points about me not having any desire to seek revenge, and my commitment to honoring God, because I actually ran into this individual about seven years after (including my Iowa time). The incident took place in Rockingham County Jail. Let me tell you, it's easy to say what you would do when forced to face your enemy, especially when you don't think that your integrity will ever be put to the test. But when thrust into a situation like that, it quickly becomes an opportunity for those around you, and God, to see where it is that your loyalty lies. Does your flesh rule and reign or is God on the throne of your heart enabling you to walk in love?

Like I said earlier though, I never had any beef with the dude, and I only carried it the way that I did because the tension in the pod made me feel like I needed to get him before he got me. So, when our paths finally did cross, there literally was no malice in my heart towards him. Plus, during those seven years, God was effectively transforming me. My time in Iowa was centered around me basically just working out, working, and participating in church activities. Of course, there was plenty of other stuff going on, but I just wasn't interested in it. I was recruited by gang members to join their organizations, and even approached about potentially starting my own by organizing the guys who fell (caught charges) from the same city I fell from. And as tempting as some of these propositions were, once God got a hold of me, there was no turning back. I was fully aware of where those roads led, and I wanted better for my family and for myself.

So, I did my best to walk the straight and narrow but still look out for those that were on a different trajectory who needed my help. God revealed many talents to me, most of which I had no idea I even possessed, and he created a platform for me to showcase these talents for the glory of His name. He increased my wisdom, my level of discernment, and taught me the power of words. Which is a subject I believe the world should take a course on, because far too often we allow our mouths to say things without fully thinking through how they may be perceived, interpreted, or what harm they might cause. And in my opinion, *that's* an extremely dangerous thing to do. The Bible states that "life and death is in the power of the tongue." So, as they say, "with great power comes great responsibility." We are to be mindful of how we go about using this power. It is strictly for the edification, motivation, education, and/or correction of those around us. In love of course.

But I said all of that to say that once I ran into this individual at Augusta Correctional Center, I was in a far better place (more mature) then I was when I last saw him. Which wasn't a bad place; I just had to make sure I protected myself. I believe I was only there a few days before I ran into him, and his response was so friendly that you would have never thought that we were once on a keep away list. In turn I addressed him with a cordial attitude. Now of course for the next couple of months when he was around, I would always proceed with care, because prison life had taught me that most people hide their true intentions until the perfect opportunity to execute their plans presents itself. All glory to God, nothing ever occurred between me and him, and the way this particular institution was run, there were plenty of chances for either of us to attempt to inflict harm on the other.

CHAPTER 17

Sentencing

It finally came time for my sentencing hearing in Virginia, and everything was set as far as who would testify for and against me. Of course, those who were set to testify against me were brought in by the prosecution to make me seem far worse than I really was, and those who volunteered to speak on my behalf strove to combat their verbal attacks by making me sound better than I actually was. We all know that the truth lies somewhere in between. I was far from a saint, but I was also not a heartless individual either, which is the portrayal that I believe screamed the loudest. Meaning that based on the time that I was sentenced to, it appeared that their depiction of me was all that the sentencing judge heard and based on that he sentenced me to the max according to my guidelines, which was 31 years. During the portion of the hearing where he was handing down my time, it appeared that he was showing leniency because even though he maxed me out on every charge (82 years), he suspended most of the time. But that was a ploy because he couldn't justly give me more time than he did, not without it backfiring on him once I appealed his decision. So, even though he expressed how "heartbroken" he was to have to give me the time that he did, while doing so it just didn't appear that it bothered him any, because he sentenced me as if I was beyond repair.

But prior to the sentencing phase, the character witnesses on both sides spoke. Before I go on, I want to thank and apologize to both sets of witnesses. I want to thank all those who made the trip to Virginia to testify on my behalf. I don't take what you did and the sacrifice that you made lightly; you could've been anywhere else in the world, yet you chose to support me, and for that I am truly grateful. At the same time though, I want to apologize for having put you in that position in the first place, you deserve far better from me, and from here on out that's what you're going to get. To the victims, I also apologize for having put you through the initial trauma of the robbery itself, and then having to relive that experience over again had to be tough. I thank you too for having enlightened me to just how deeply my actions affected you, the pain that I felt that day based on the pain that you expressed is something I never want to experience again, and I pray you never do either.

I also was afforded the opportunity to speak on my own behalf, but in the midst of all my tears, I could barely get out that which I had spent a hefty amount of time preparing. If my words were lost on the crowd, at least my remorse shined through. In my written statement though, I highlighted the passage where the religious leaders brought an adulterous woman before Christ to entrap him by speaking to the fact that according to the law of Moses the woman should be put to death, asking what He had to say about the matter.

Christ responded by saying, "Let he who is without sin cast the first stone," then kneeling down he began writing in the sand, and slowly, one by one, all the accusers of the woman started to fade away.

Then Christ asked the woman, "Woman, where are your accusers"?

To which she replied, "They are no more."

Finally, Christ pardoned the woman by saying, "Neither do I accuse you, go and sin no more."

Now, of course, I didn't believe that by me referencing this story I wouldn't do any time, but I did hope that God would use it to move on the heart of the judge and have him show a little leniency. Instead, the book was thrown at me, and not the good book I might add. A fact that I didn't fully come to realize until I was back in the holding cell of the courthouse, where my lawyer came in and explained how much time I received. Instantly my heart dropped, and the sense of this came over me, as if me spending the majority of my adult life in prison was how the storybook ended, leaving no future for me. And the possibility of that being the storyline attached to me whenever I was thought of crushed me inside. As to not put my family in a position where they felt like they had to worry more than they already did, I just held it in and put on a brave face.

So, I finally got back to the pod and was greeted by those whom I was doing time with, and they proceeded to ask me what happened. I unfortunately had to express that the outcome was not what I/we (me and my family) had hoped for. Following that conversation with them, I immediately went to my cell to spend some time alone, because although I knew what the situation was, it still all kind of felt like a dream. And out of respect, the fellas in there with me who were genuinely heartbroken by how much time they gave me, gave me a good hour or so to be by myself before they all came to check in on me, at which point I broke down in tears while they attempted to console me. It had just gotten to the point that I couldn't hold it any longer once the thoughts of not being able to take part in the lives of those that I love poured in, at least not in the way that I now wanted to be. Prior to that point, I have to admit that I took that/them for granted.

Now, with my family and friends, was the only place that I wanted to be. For the next couple of days, thoughts of life without them, especially my daughter who I believe was still 3 years old at the time, consumed me, preventing me from even enjoying my workouts, because in the middle of doing pushups, I would break down in tears.

I'm not sure how long that lasted, but it's all thanks to God that I even got through it, and sober at that, because they tried to offer me some form of medication (I'm guessing to help me sleep) after my sentencing to help me cope with the time. I refused, of course, feeling as if I had all I needed in my relationship with Christ, and I didn't trust taking anything from anyone who had any affiliation with the judicial system, even the nurses. I'm still that way to this day; they just came around offering flu shots to all those who wanted them, and I refused that for the very reason that I refused the medication offered in the jail. After my sentencing was over, I didn't remain in Virginia much longer, but for the week or so that I was there, waiting to be transported back to Iowa, I had a really important conversation take place that would shape my perspective on the importance of setting a Godly example for those around you.

The circumstances which led to the conversation went as follows: I was in the pod discussing the importance of remaining faithful and staying the course in regard to your relationship with Christ regardless of the difficulties in life that you will inevitably face. And after I finished discussing that with the guys, I proceeded to head to my cell and was subsequently followed by one of the inmates that was not a part of the discussion but had overheard it. Once we reached my cell, I sat down, and he went on to express how the level of commitment I had to honoring God with my life inspired him to embark on his own spiritual journey, and that he had been watching me closely ever since my sentencing occurred to see how I would respond since things didn't go my way. Would I continue to trust God? Or would I surrender my faith and revert back to doing things my own way?

These were the two options that I faced, and little did I know that the choice that I made would have implications far greater than I assumed. Fortunately, I chose what would prove to be the second-best decision of my life (the first being accepting Christ in the first place), and I hoped to set the stage for the individual that I was speaking with at my cell that day to move forward in pursuing a life governed by Christ, and as a result do some really great things.

He testified that it did just that. He said that at that point had I walked away from my faith, then he would have too, and there's no telling how many lives connected to the call that God has on his life would have been negatively affected had I and he given up on God.

To be honest, that's an extremely intimidating thing to think about, the responsibility that we bear to consistently do and say what is pleasing in the eyes of God, and that what we do and say has the ability to motivate or discourage someone to or not to continue in the faith. But thankfully we are not alone in this, Christ upon His departure to heaven left us the 'comforter', which is the Holy Spirit, that enables us to exercise self-control and be obedient to the Word of the Lord even when it is not easy to do so.

CHAPTER 18

Impact Players

So, I left Virginia with a deeper understanding of the potential impact (good or bad) that I could have on the lives of those around me. I also attempted to have a conversation with a woman that played a major role in my life from my freshman year at Virginia Tech up until about two and a half years into my Iowa bid, but at that time she was still in shock (understandably so) and wasn't ready to discuss the possibility of our relationship coming to an end. Which I really wanted to do at that time because I didn't believe that our relationship (or anyone else's relationship for that matter) could survive the amount of time that I was sentenced to do. But because she expressed that she wasn't ready, I didn't press her to do so. I simply said that eventually we would have to revisit this topic, but until then as long as she desired to be a part of my life, I wouldn't push her away. Like I said though, I had no faith in us making it, at least initially, but over time as she consistently supported me emotionally and financially, I began to feel that we could possibly be the exception to the rule. Long story short, that turned out not to be the case.

About two and a half years in she realized that it was far more difficult to love someone in my situation then she thought, and as a result, she felt it best that we go our separate ways. This affected me far more than I thought it ever would. I hadn't realized how much faith I had put into this person to be someone that I would forever be able to count on, yet she was the first person to turn their back on me. Even still, I hold no ill will in my heart against her, I still love and pray for her as often as I remember, and anywhere down the road if she finds herself in a tough spot and needs my help I would gladly lend a hand. I would like to thank her for the time that she and my other homegirls were able to hang in there, because at the end of the day, they owed me nothing, and for the time that they did show love, they gave me everything.

There are two females in particular that I would really like to highlight, the first is my lady friend Mercedes. She has been the most incredible friend that any man could ever ask for and hasn't asked for or demanded anything in return. The only thing she ever expected of me was that I reciprocate the love and respect that she has consistently shown me, which for an individual such as myself love, loyalty, and respect shown to those that keep it all the way real with me goes without saying. So, because of that, me and her are 'thick as thieves' till this very day. I couldn't imagine not having her as my friend, and I've committed myself to being there for her until the day that I am no longer here on earth.

The other woman would be my homegirl/ex-fiancé, Elizabeth Dawn. She is also an extremely incredible woman and friend, so much so that for two plus years, I considered the option of making her my wife. This was a really big deal when coming from me because of the fact that I expressed earlier about not believing in penitentiary relationships, and also the standards that I have that my potential wife must reach are extremely high and often disqualify most women before we ever get anywhere close to discussing marriage. But in her, I found someone who I know without a shadow of a doubt loves me completely, and who would sacrifice all that she has to see to it that what we were working towards at that time would be accomplished. Any man would be lucky to have her as his wife, and for that reason I find it very unfortunate that our level of compatibility wasn't higher, because due to that fact I had to cause her pain by ending our relationship, which in turn caused me pain as well. But thankfully at this point, and regardless of us not being together, we are still friends, and hopefully we will be until the end of time.

And of course, there were a few more who popped in and out throughout my bid, and their presence was appreciated also, but as in professional sports, there are some who are 'impact players' and some that are not. And those that are viewed as such are usually those that come through in the clutch when the game is tight, and you need a big play. By doing so on a consistent basis, they embroider their names alongside those that will be remembered forever. And Betsy and Mercedes are definitely two of my impact players.

CHAPTER 19

O.G. & Fort Dodge, Iowa

Once I got back to Iowa from Virginia, I spent about a week in the Fort Dodge receiving center before being transported to prison. Prior to my departure I had already spent about 30 days in Iowa and had already been processed. When it did come time for me to go, I was cuffed and placed in a transport van with about four other inmates. There was one in particular that stood out from among the rest because he seemingly had a special glow around him. I mean one of those Last Dragon 'Who's the master?' glows. I think he caught me staring at him, and that's what compelled him to speak. He said hello, introduced himself, and asked me if I was a church goer. I replied by saying yes, and from that moment on we became friends, or better yet, brothers in the Lord. I immediately began to view him as the spiritual father that I was so in need of, because me being so young in the faith and this being my first bid, I really had no clue what walking my faith out in the confines of the penitentiary was supposed to look like.

In the prison we were in, they had a level system in place, where every 60 to 90 days you were evaluated, and if you were able to remain charge free, you would be approved to move up to the next level. So, being that me and my spiritual father, O.G. arrived at the same time, we were able to move up in the level system together, which granted me a front row seat to watch him go about his daily business. I was able to see how often he read and prayed, and also how he handled conflict, which wasn't always in the way that most might classify as 'righteous'. But when he erred in judgment, he quickly forgave himself, knowing that he had already been forgiven by God, and he continued to press forward toward the mark. This was a major lesson for me because being a young believer, I put an enormous amount of pressure on myself to be perfect in my walk with Christ. When I would fail, I would sometimes mentally beat myself up for days. This led to me feeling so ashamed for having sinned against God, that I would attempt to hide from him like Adam did in the garden of Eden after eating from the tree that God forbade him to. I would not pray or study His Word. Like Adam, I felt unworthy in my nakedness before God, not truly understanding the depth of the love that He had for me, that in my time of weakness He wanted nothing more than to commune with me, and that by being honest about my frailties, His strength was then made perfect in my weakness.

Me and O.G. were able to move up in levels together. There were five of them, but we stopped at level four because we had gotten comfortable 'doing time' around the guys that were there with us. Usually together was me, O.G., N.O. (my blood homie from New Orleans), and Mr. Johnson (who I believe was in his early seventies). And during our leisure time, if me or O.G. didn't have church, we would all play dominoes or spades together to entertain ourselves. By leisure time I mean when we didn't all have to work. I only bring our church attendance up though because that's how we spent most of our time, which is another thing that rubbed off on me from O.G. He spent as much time as he could fellowshipping with other Christian brothers, and also helping out the chaplain with whatever was needed of him. So, in turn, I did the same thing, which really helped expedite my spiritual maturation process because when you are as young in the faith as I was, I really believe it to be paramount to your growth to be surrounded by those who exemplify what it means to be men or women of God. That will also support you in your walk when you 'fail'.

To me, that support is vital because one thing that you will have no problem finding once you openly profess to be a Christian is someone to criticize your walk. Individuals that will love and support you unconditionally are rare. Once your profession has been made, or allegiance clarified, it seems that instantly everyone around you becomes an expert on how living your faith out is supposed to look, even those who may not even be living according to the word of God themselves. They all attempt to box you in and control your life by imposing their interpretation of what the word of the Lord says on you, not understanding that the revelation given through the Holy Spirit is based on where you are in life (positionally) and what you're going through (mentally, physically, spiritually, and emotionally), and because of that, the application of the revelation given may vary.

There is a quote that says, "You should be firm in your principles, but flexible in your approach." That to me is the epitome of what the Christian life is all about, that just because we may find ourselves in similar situations, that does not mean that the spirit of the Lord is necessarily going to lead us to handle that situation the same way. There are several instances in the Bible where men of God found themselves involved in similar scenarios more than a few times (mostly when facing an impending battle). And when they petitioned the Lord for His guidance in regard to what to do and how to go about doing it, He rarely dished out the same formula twice. So, for all of you young believers out there, it's cool to seek wise counsel from those who you respect in the faith, and I encourage you to strongly consider what they have to say prior to making whatever decision lies ahead.

Ultimately your guidance should come from the Father above. Christ has left us the Holy Spirit whose responsibility is to 'guide us into all truth', and that truth, as it pertains to your struggle, which comes directly from God, may sound strange to those who are not going through what you're going through based on their own experience with God (or the lack thereof) in a seemingly similar circumstance.

God gave Joseph a dream for his future, and he was criticized for sharing it by the very people he loved, and he thought loved him the most, simply because they couldn't fathom God elevating Joseph to the extent that those who were older and therefore deemed more important would one day bow at his feet. I'm pretty sure that if you reflect back on your life, you can think of someone who may have said something that discouraged you from pursuing something you were passionate about because they felt like you didn't have what it takes to be successful in that arena, or that's not what they had in mind for you. You know sometimes parents attempt to live through their kids. If you allow them to, people will attempt to define you by and limit you to the environment you were born into or the mistakes that you've made. As if that's all you'll ever be, all because they don't possess the ability to see the vision that God has given you.

Take King David for example. He was created to be king of Israel and also slay Goliath. Yet when he inquired about the reward for doing so, his older brothers mocked him for leaving his sheep. They knew that he was anointed to do great things based on the prophet Samuel's visit, where each of them was found not to be the chosen one of God and David was. And still they refused to view him as anything other than a shepherd boy. Thankfully in both cases they ignored those that would have them settle for less than God's best, or attempt to quench the fire within them, and as a result they both fulfilled their destiny.

Me and O.G. were also blessed to have been able to maintain employment our entire time together. God was gracious in using the facility to help aid us in obtaining the things that we needed in order to do time more comfortably. Of course, the jobs we had didn't provide us with much money, and there were things that we wanted but couldn't afford, but throughout our time in Fort Dodge together, I can't remember a time when we were deprived of the necessities (hygiene and the like). Our situation was similar to that in the Book of Acts where the church (or body of believers) provided for each other by selling everything they owned. They then brought the proceeds to the elders of the church to distribute to those that were in need. Everything me and O.G. had, we shared, and I believe that it was due to our generosity towards one another (not to mention those around us), that similar to the woman during the famine that was obedient to the prophet by baking him something to eat first, our "vats" (or boxes) never went dry.

God was extremely faithful to me and taught me early on in my bid that he was and forever would be my provider. Even going as far as blessing me with what was my penitentiary dream job that also paid more money and afforded me basically unlimited access to the gymnasium to work out. This was a job that everyone on the compound coveted, and one that although I hoped to get one day, I knew was a long shot. But God, who is the creator of all things, and a reward of those that diligently seek him, provided me with favor with an older guy that held the position I desired and so happened to be on his way home. I was able to develop a relationship with this individual simply because he oversaw the weight pit, and I spent an enormous amount of my time there. I even would sometimes stop by on the way to the gym or church when I didn't plan on working out. So, for an intelligent individual such as he was, it wasn't hard to see that I possessed a passion for fitness, and as a result of our limited dialogue it appeared, based on his recommendation to the gym staff, that I was also someone that he had grown fond of as a person.

In order for him to feel confident enough to suggest me as his successor, he had developed the reputation of being a quality worker therefore gaining favor with the gym supervisors. When he mentioned that he thought that I would be a quality replacement, they called me right in for an interview. This was basically a formality because they had already made up in their mind that they were going to give me the position. I remind you of how popular this gig was, and that I never filled out an application for the job, so I wasn't even on the waiting list, but that's how it goes when you have the favor of God in your life. Now, if I stopped this particular story/testimony right there, it would be more than enough to shout about, but I would be doing you a grave disservice if I failed to express to you that there is a flip side to this coin, and that side bares the label of obedience.

The other reason that I received the job in the fashion that I did was that once the gym supervisors heard my name, it rang a bell because they had already taken notice of me while refereeing the flag football league. They took notice of my God given size and athleticism of course, but more importantly than that, they got to witness my character under pressure. Meaning how I conduct myself when things aren't going my way, which I believe any kind of team sport is the best testing ground for character because you can only control your performance. So, frustration in my opinion is inevitable, either because you didn't perform at the level you're accustomed to so you're down on yourself, or you did and still came out with a loss due to one of your teammates not pulling their weight. Either way, how you respond says a lot about you, and fortunately for me, in most cases I was able to handle myself maturely, therefore causing the supervisors to view me in a positive light. And for that all praise goes to the most High, the great I Am, the creator of heaven and earth, the author and finisher of my faith. Because had it not been for the work that he had done in me up until that point, I would've surely disqualified myself from being a viable candidate for the position that I received.

Case in point, I remember a game where I almost lost it (mentally); we were the number one team at the time and with that often comes jealousy, which breeds contempt, so a lot of people wanted to see us lose. And on this particular day things really weren't going our way, from our performance as a team to the calls by the referees, it appeared that although we were the superior team, the opposition was going to get the better of us. So, frustration was starting to set in, and if you ask any competitive athlete, when you're not performing at your best and are losing the game at the same time, the last thing you want to hear is trash talk. So, I'm lined up near the far sideline waiting for the ball to be hiked so I could run my route and someone from the bleachers started to heckle me, and based on what was taking place, and had already taken place, I was in my feelings and wasn't feeling him. As a result, I attempted to blurt something back at him that was extremely unholy, but when my mouth opened, it was as if I had lost my voice, for no words came out. It was like the Holy Spirit confiscated my tongue for that crucial moment, rendering me mute, as to keep me from turning an insignificant situation (based on the big picture of my life) into something that at that time would have pushed back my parole had it gone south.

I often describe that situation as God saving me from myself, which I'm so thankful that He did, because outside of that incident, my time there went fairly smoothly. Other than the heartbreak I spoke of when my 'first lady' walked out on me, there was no real pain attached to my bid there. Of course, everybody misses their freedom and family, but once you get into the rhythm of doing time, you really don't think about the streets as often as most might think. To be honest, once I got into the flow of things, it really didn't hit me that I was locked up until I was about two years removed from the streets. I remember standing out in front of the unit I resided in with O.G., performing my occupational duties and surveying the compound, when it hit me like a ton of bricks.

I looked at O.G. and said, "Man, I'm locked up."

He responded by saying, "You just now figuring that out?"

I'm sure that that's how most of you would have responded too had you been in his position. Which I completely understand because it does sound a bit strange, me just coming to that realization having already served a little over two years. But like I said earlier while explaining my sentencing process, everything was happening so fast that the majority of it felt like a dream at times. But the thing that I believe played the greatest role in me not realizing it sooner was that I immediately met O.G., submerged myself in the word of God (either through my personal studies or through my church attendance), and therefore proved true the scripture that says, "I will keep him in perfect peace whose mind is stayed on me." And that's just what God did.

CHAPTER 20

Brothers in Faith

As I committed myself to being obedient to His word and setting a Godly example for those around me, God kept me shielded from the chaos that was my environment. I was often somewhat oblivious to what was going on around me, even though I was well connected and fully aware. It's just that while there (and still till this day), I took the "road less travelled" so I rarely experienced any collisions with those that were travelling in the opposite direction. It's kind of like travelling on the highway where there's a median in the middle, and in prison (just like on the highway), it's much safer to stay in your lane, so most individuals do. And that's not to say that I didn't often make myself available to them, because I had plenty of guys there that weren't my brothers in the faith that I rocked with, but unless we were discussing something of importance (faith, family, or our future plans), those interactions were short and sweet. Then it was, as Christ would say, back to being about my Father's business. Because that was from which my joy, peace, and fulfillment came, and at that time, I couldn't see any better way to do my bid.

I admired how the church community operated there, doing certain things such as the passing out of cards during Christmas time, and also yearly putting on a Christian weekend retreat that was available to all, designed to introduce nonbelievers to the faith and help those young in the faith to grow. It also afforded those who had already gone through it, and that had developed a certain level of maturity for having done so, an opportunity to serve. This retreat lasted four days, and I describe it as a retreat because it was similar to a spiritual getaway, where you were able to physically surround yourself with other believers who genuinely wanted to become more like Christ and emotionally connect with others that were on the fence about whether fighting the good fight of faith was the path that they should take. It was a getaway from the chaos that we found ourselves in daily, where even if you weren't experiencing the worst of the storm, you still got a bit wet from the rain, meaning that even though you avoided certain affiliations or didn't participate in certain activities that could potentially put you in harm's way, nobody gets through a prison bid unscathed.

But in that environment, you were able to lay down all your burdens at the foot of God's throne and focus solely on the creator himself, which is something that, as we mature, we should develop the habit of doing regardless of our surroundings or circumstance. God is forever commanding us to cast our cares on Him so that we can experience the freedom attached to truly knowing that which concerns us is in the best hands possible, therefore we can expect the best outcome imaginable. The Bible says that "It's impossible to please God without faith," and "Faith comes by the hearing of the word of God." So, for the entire weekend retreat, you took part in what could be referred to as a scriptural baptism, where the word of God was not only made plain so that those who were in a place to receive it could do so confidently, but it was also exemplified by those who governed the retreat as to make the transition from hearing to doing what the word of God commands a smooth one.

They also had a leadership committee whose role was to answer the requests of the inmate population and provide the chaplain and guest teachers with whatever assistance they needed to ensure that the service went off without a hitch. They also were expected to serve as Christ ambassadors to the entire population, but especially to the brothers in the faith by sharing the Gospel with the lost and supporting those in their walk-in whatever way they needed. Whether it was through providing a bar of soap, words of encouragement, or a shoulder to lean on, they performed the role that the disciples played back in Jesus' day. Because of the direct access to the chaplain that you received, and how freely you were able to move about the compound, being a part of the leadership committee was something that individuals coveted.

Due to their extreme desire to hold the title of LC member, oftentimes they would play politics in order to be placed in line for a potential spot when it was available. This meant that they would underhandedly develop relationships with those who were on the committee solely for the purpose of a recommendation, as opposed to genuinely wanting to "study at the feet" or be mentored by the individual to which they cleaved. And those practices I know God wasn't pleased with, and fortunately nor did they ever appeal to me, I was (as well as O.G.) fully content with being where I was and operating at the level of anointing that God had bestowed upon me, based on Him knowing what I could handle, until He decided to promote me. I wasn't going to swindle my way into any position regardless of the perks that were attached to it. Somehow, I subconsciously knew that it was important for me to be patient with the process of developing the Christlike character that would eventually enable me to represent the position of LC member at a consistently high level. Because like I spoke to earlier while describing my time in Rockingham county jail, the example we set for those who are looking on can have an enormous effect on how they view the Christian faith and could potentially sway them towards or away from the faith.

So instead of diabolically going about the business of positioning ourselves to be a part of the council, we instead chose to serve simply for the purpose of striving to honor God with the time allotted to us, meaning every second of every day that God provided us with air to breathe we only wanted to do and say that which Christ would be pleased with. If there was work, to be done, we were willing and happy to do it, because at that time (and still to this day), in my eyes, it was an honor and a privilege to be considered a vessel worthy of use by God. Based on our faithful service, eventually (and I'd like to add inevitably), we were asked to join the council. And based on the fact that we felt like it was a sign from God that he wanted to increase our influence, we accepted. It was an honor that we both took very seriously because we knew that it came with great responsibility.

As the saying goes, "To whom much is given much is required." To a certain extent, we knew what that involved as it pertained to the duties of the council, which was reaching out to the inmate community and setting a Godly example. But little did we know that we were really about to learn what it meant to lay down our lives for Christ, and experience what it felt like to be persecuted for doing so, therefore sharing in his suffering.

CHAPTER 21

Fallen

A perfect example is that not long after me and O.G. joined the council, another available spot opened up. As is the normal procedure, the council came together to discuss the possibility of filling the vacant spot and nominate people to potentially fill it. There were a few potential candidates that in my opinion would have been great choices, but after careful deliberation, the council agreed on this heavyset black guy that me and O.G. didn't know, and therefore weren't even aware that he was a part of the Christian community. While in my limited experience at the time, us having no knowledge of this individual as being as active as we were wasn't a good sign; it just appeared that this individual had not yet proven himself faithful enough through his service to others to have been a candidate for the position. I was only interested in voting members in that I felt would boldly stand on and for the word of God. Meaning that the same fire that they exhibited during praise and worship while surrounded by other believers, they would also exhibit on the yard while attempting to win souls for our heavenly father. Which is a critical point to make because so many of us born again believers would much rather cling to our Bibles and hide within the four walls of our homes or churches, as opposed to venturing out into the areas that need our help the most.

We operate with a high level of timidity, fearful of our testimony not being received well by those who we minister to. And we allow that fear to hinder us from boldly sharing our faith, even while knowing that the Bible says, "God has not given us the spirit of fear, but of power, love, and a sound mind." So, we are to share our faith in faith, knowing that God is with us, and because of that in all things we are more than conquerors. Now that doesn't guarantee that the "lost soul" will receive the message that you deliver, but the joy or satisfaction that you receive from boldly stepping out for the glory of His name can't be matched by anything that this world has to offer. And living in fear hinders you from experiencing all that Christ has in store for those who believe.

This individual was told of his induction and moving forward it was business as usual. To be honest, I don't remember ever really seeing or interacting with this guy, even after he was voted in. Not due to me avoiding or not having a desire to, but if I remember correctly, he was just never around, which further validates me feeling as if he shouldn't have been voted on in the first place. This is a vital mistake that many people make when choosing a life partner, thinking that added responsibilities that come along with being married or having children will somehow help motivate them to improve upon their behavior instead of believing them to be who they reveal themselves to be prior to entering into these life altering commitments. This individual was rarely around prior to him becoming a part of the committee, so what led those who voted for him to believe that attaching a title to his name would change anything?

Not long after this individual had been voted in, it was discovered that he was actively participating in homosexual activities, which is frowned upon in the Christian community, and is a sin that the Bible refers to as being an abomination. So, you can probably guess what happened next. An investigation was started to see if the allegations were true, and once they were corroborated by several other witnesses, a council meeting was then called. In this council meeting, we as brothers joined hands to pray and seek God's guidance, then upon the conclusion of prayer, we opened the word of God to see what it was that God had already said concerning such an offense even though it was pretty much widely known what God's feelings are concerning sin, particularly this sin. Yet still, it was important that we revisit the scriptures to not allow our personal biases to taint the process. Once the word of God was read, the Council discussed what it was that needed to be done. Do we reprimand the individual in hopes that he recognized the error in his behavior and therefore from that point on flew straight? Or remove him from the council completely, operating under a zero-tolerance policy?

The conversation went on for what seemed like hours as valid points for both solutions were made. In the end though, based on majority votes, it was agreed upon that this council member would be asked to step down. There would be no attention drawn to his removal, nor would we speak to the reason behind his removal if anyone were to ask. We did not want any drama attached to this situation, neither did we desire to embarrass him. Due to his displeasure at being removed, he went to the authorities (sergeant, captain, or major) with a discrimination complaint. And because of his complaint, they ambushed us after one of our services, taking all those that were a part of the council to a private room in the facility to wait to be questioned by their investigator. But, of course, at the time we were clueless as to why we were being detained and did not figure out what was actually going on until the first of us was escorted away and then returned to share what they had gone through.

One by one we were taken aside for questioning, and one by one we all came back rejoicing that God had counted us righteous enough to suffer for His name's sake. Because at the end of the day, the reason that we were being chastised was because we had stood firmly on our faith, and therefore removed someone from our council who wasn't as adamant about doing so. Finally, the questioning was done due to the fact that they ran out of council members to interrogate, and upon the conclusion of their inquiry, our motives were found to be righteous, therefore protecting us from having to endure the punishment for having done what we were accused of. Which was discriminating against the fallen council member simply based on his sexual preference just for the sake of doing so, which was the farthest thing from the truth.

We had not banned this individual from attending Christian services; we just expressed that at this time, he would not be able to hold a leadership position, feeling that continuing to allow him to do so would set a bad precedent. We were considered (as I spoke to earlier) to be God's anointed apostles, sent forth to share the gospel with all those who were strangers to the faith and called to be the light of the world/salt of the earth. This is not to imply that any of us were above reproach, but there was a certain level of maturity that had to be exhibited to the inmate community from those attached to the council. To the best of our ability and through the power of the Holy Spirit we were to at all times strive to glorify and honor God by being obedient to his word.

CHAPTER 22

Parole

My stay in Iowa was not long at all, but I have to say that it was productive as it pertains to the increase of my faith; God strengthened and used me in incredible ways.

Before I left, I also experienced disappointment attached to me evangelizing and mentoring two young men that God led across my path. I refuse to go into too much detail concerning all the time that was spent by me investing in these two (simply because it's not about me), which I was more than happy to do because I considered helping them my reasonable service. But the short story is that they came into the knowledge of who God is, and I felt led to commit myself to their physical and spiritual growth. So, we began to work out and spend time together, getting to know each other. As a result of it, progress was definitely being made on both fronts (physically and spiritually) during their stay at Fort Dodge Correctional Center. But once these individuals were released to the street, I received word that they had both regressed, falling back into old bad habits.

My heart ached when I received the news, much like a father or mothers' heart would ache if their child had gone astray by choosing a path that they felt like wouldn't facilitate their future success. I wanted nothing more than for them to experience God's best for their lives, and at that time, I felt like they would potentially never receive all that God had in store for them because of how strong of a hold it appeared that the enemy had on them.

But once I was able to get past the disappointment and guilt linked to my guy's shortcomings and feeling like I should've done more, I was then reminded by the Holy Spirit that God is the "author and finisher" of their faith, and that which He began in them, He would see through to completion. So, there was no reason for me to obsess over that which I had no control over. They committed their lives to Christ while incarcerated, and I committed them to Christ once they departed. Prior to and upon their release they were in the best hands possible, and because of that fact, I am fully confident that if they aren't already back on track, they will be eventually. My God is just amazing like that.

I went up before the parole board as scheduled, not really knowing what to expect being that it was my first prison bid, and therefore my first parole hearing. Only having witnessed other guys going up (never talking to any), I basically did what I saw them do, which was shave and dress as if they were going to a job interview. Which would seem to be common sense; of course, you want to look presentable as you stand before the people who are in charge of your freedom. But you'd be surprised how different some people approach their parole process.

We were all asked to wait in a class until it was our turn, and when our turn arrived, we were then escorted into another private room where we were sat in front of a tv screen. On the screen was the parole board. How many I can't recall, but there was this sweet middle-aged black woman who did all of the talking. She and my mom were about the same age and even resembled each other, which is one of the reasons I think I felt so at ease. The main reason I felt at ease though was that I was fully confident that God was with me. On top of that, I had fulfilled every rehabilitation requirement they placed on me coming in. So there really was no reason for them not to free me, but then again I didn't see the need for the judge in Virginia to give me all the time that he did, yet God still allowed it. So there really was no telling what the outcome would be.

I was asked a series of questions by the woman I described, none of which were connected to the crimes that I was incarcerated for in Iowa. Instead, she asked me about the robberies that I committed in Virginia. To be honest, that caught me a bit off guard. Even still, I strove to answer the questions as fluidly and eloquently as I could. I was completely honest about the state of mind that I was in during that period of my life, and then testified to the man that God had transformed me into throughout the time I spent at F.D.C.C.

The spirit of God was definitely in that place giving power to that which I said, because for the parole woman to speak to me the way that she did once the interview was done was nothing short of amazing. She went on to say that in spite of the poor choices that I had made, she had no doubt in her mind that if and when given the opportunity I could be a model citizen. This was very encouraging for me as a young believer to hear, because it was evidence that God was with me (in spite of all the disappointment I experienced during my court proceedings in Virginia), and the work that He was doing in me was real.

But after she said what she said, she told me that I was granted parole, and she wished me luck as I continued on this journey we all call life. It now became a waiting game, me waiting and praying that Virginia decided that it was way too expensive to fly to and from Iowa just for little ole me. And if I remember correctly, they only had about thirty business days to do so before I would then be released. So,

I waited, and waited, and waited, praying that this would be the opportunity that God took to deliver me from this bondage. I wanted so badly to be at home.

But Virginia ended up coming. They did, and while they were happy about it, I was not. Still, I was determined to trust God, understanding that if He didn't see fit to release me at that time, then it was either because I wasn't ready, or the circumstances on the outside had yet to align. Either way His decision as it pertains to my freedom was motivated by love and centered around what was best for me.

CHAPTER 23

Mindful of the Weak

So, to Virginia I went. They came to get me on pretty much the last day within the time that was allotted to them. And just as before, we flew, but only this time it was on the governor's private plane. Yep, you heard me correctly. These people were so thirsty to get me back in their custody to do this absurd amount of time that they had sentenced me to, that they gassed up the governor's private jet. I was escorted by two U.S. marshals who fed me a pretty decent Subway meal on the way and attempted to engage me in small talk. I really wasn't in the mood for all that.

Once we touched down in Virginia, I was immediately taken to one of their receiving centers to be housed and processed. This varies in regard to how long that process actually takes, but I was only there for about 30 days, thankfully.

Why thankfully you ask?

Because there was no air conditioning in that facility, and it was in the middle of spring. Not to mention that each cell had a hot water pipe in it, which added more heat to an already miserably hot situation. I'm talking so hot that me and my cell partner would strip down to our boxers and take turns sitting at the door where there was a little airflow from a fan they placed in the middle of the walkway outside the cell. When I look back on it, the only cool thing about it was that you had somebody to kind of suffer through it with, someone who understood what it was that you were going through because they were going through it too.

So, to deal with it, you find different ways to take your mind off it, crack jokes to make light of it, and pray that your stay isn't as long as some of the others that you've heard about. It was also a wild place because there were barely any cameras in the portion of the receiving center that I was in, so you can imagine what kinda craziness took place while the hardest of criminals operated pretty much unsupervised. There was a time while I was there that this young guy randomly came to my cell sporting a black eye expressing that he just kept getting into fights and he didn't know why. Or asking me how to get whoever was beating on him to stop, and although I felt for the young brother, I didn't feel spirit led to come to his defense. Which may sound strange to you after reading about how I came to the aid of the older white guy while in county jail, and I can understand that thought process, but what I don't believe that you are factoring in is that within these walls, you constantly have to be aware of individuals attempting to manipulate you.

Whether most may agree with it or not, in prison there are certain actions that provoke a certain response that many on the outside may consider to be heinous or a bit overboard yet are considered justified by the majority of inmates. There are certain unwritten laws that you just don't violate, and once an individual does, there are consequences that then follow (in most cases). What cowardly individuals do is knowingly violate these laws, and once a certain amount of pressure has been applied by the person that they've transgressed against, they run to someone like me. They play as if they are clueless as to why such trouble has befallen them, all in hopes that I would sympathize with what they're going through, and as a result intervene. They attempt to play on my faith, knowing love and mercy are two Godly attributes that I strive to extend to all those that I come in contact with. But at the same time, they fail to understand that I also believe a man should assume responsibility for his actions and be able to stand in the face of whatever the penalty is based on the decisions that he makes.

I'm not into coddling grown men, nor enabling behavior that I view to be reckless. The Bible clearly states that "that which a man/woman soweth, that shall he or she also reap," so who am I to step in the way of God's divine order of things? Now, if it's clearly a situation such as the story I told you concerning the older gentleman I aided in Rockingham County Jail, where he had done nothing to warrant the mistreatment of the inmates surrounding him, then in those situations, it's incumbent upon me to do like the Bible states and "be mindful of the weak." And when I'm approached by people lobbying for my help, it's important for me to be sensitive to the leading of the Holy Spirit, because only the spirit of God can accurately discern the hearts and motives of men. So no, I did not assist this young man in coming up with a solution to his problem because (1) I didn't know the ins and outs of all that was going on, and (2) my heart never felt moved to act on his behalf.

I only had three cellmates while I was there (which is rare because the turnover rate is so high), and I got along with all of them really well. One was this Hispanic guy that spoke little English, but we were able to communicate pretty well. That's the one that I spoke about when I said me and my celly had to strip down and rotate turns sitting at the door. I also (while in the cell with him) had to be the unfortunate bearer of bad news when he received some mail from immigration expressing that he would be deported once the time that he was sentenced to was completed. He was devastated, which is what made having to be the one to tell him so difficult. He had a girlfriend here that he spoke very highly of, and I think she was the major reason he didn't want to go back. He also appeared to genuinely not know that if you come into this country illegally and commit a crime, once found guilty, you become a candidate for deportation. And although I'm not sure what he did to get incarcerated, based on his reaction to the news, it's safe to say that had he known, he might have thought twice before doing what he did.

The other cellmate was this white guy who came only about a week before they packed me up. He was an okay dude and was the first person I ever made a meal with, which in prison is a way that you show the guys that you deal with that you really rock with them. You all chip in by providing different commissary items (depending on what you decide to make), someone cooks (or everyone cooks), and you all sit down together to enjoy your creation. So, yeah, me and dude got along okay.

The last cell partner I had was a young Muslim guy who I actually got a chance to engage in some deep dialogue even though technically we didn't know each other well. I can't tell you how it happened, except God created an environment where me and this young Muslim guy felt comfortable enough to fully open up about our faith, family, and future plans moving forward. As a result, I was able to share many of the incredible things that God had done for me and explain why I chose Christianity when there are obviously so many others out there. But that's kind of how evangelism goes, with the first two cellmates I had, there was never an opportunity that I could remember where I could have slid Christ into the conversation without seeming pushy, or as if I was attempting to force my faith on them. Yet the last one before I left, faith was basically all we talked about, and it happened organically, so you know that it was spirit led.

During my thirty-day orientation I met with my counselor to discuss how the point system worked and what camp I would be going to next. I only had two choices at that time because my points were so high; I was considered a level 5 security inmate, which means I had to go to a level 5 max security prison. This confused me at first, because when I thought of a max prison, I assumed that that's where murderers and those who caused havoc everywhere else they've been, would go, not someone who committed crimes where no one was hurt (well physically harmed). But based on my crimes, age, and the time I had to do, I was considered to be just as dangerous as those who committed the most heinous of crimes.

◆

CHAPTER 24

Sussex 1

So, I chose to go to Sussex 1 State Penitentiary because of the recommendation of my counselor who I believed had worked there, or he worked at the other level 5 option I had and said he thought that Sussex would provide me with a smoother transition to my bid.

The first day that I arrived, the institution was on full lockdown due to the fact that a guy had just gotten stabbed. Guess whose cell they moved me to? Yep, the very same cell that the victim lived in prior to the incident, and of course, I use that term *victim* loosely because I don't actually know whether or not he did anything to warrant the attack. But based on the experience I had with his old cellmate, and my new one, he probably considered it a blessing to get out of there, even though the way it happened wasn't pleasant.

From the very first day I knew that we weren't going to be anything close to friends, and between him and the fact that I learned that being on lock was a common theme there, I made up my mind that I most certainly had to get me a TV. But the pod as a whole was pretty cool. I ended up linking up with another guy from Florida that I was introduced to, and he quickly became a close associate of mine. We immediately began to spend the majority of our time together, and our interactions would range from working out to reminiscing about our times back home in Florida. He was an extremely intelligent individual who loved to read and was always in search of a get rich quick scheme. His vocabulary was ridiculously extensive, so much so that I would often ask him to either explain himself or tone down his speech when speaking to me. I often expressed to him that as smart as he was and as good of a heart as he had he would never be able to have the impact that he desired to have in the lives of those around him if no one could understand what it was he was trying to say.

But despite my attempt to get him to water down his dialogue, he continued to stay true to who it was he had developed himself into, a move that I will forever applaud him. (1) because he refused to dumb himself down to make others feel more comfortable with their perceived inadequacies, and (2) as a result, he then forced those around him to elevate their commitment level to developing themselves intellectually. Or at least that's what it did for me; he inspired me to grow both physically and intellectually, all by pushing me harder than I ever had been before. And for that I am truly thankful, in the short time that we were at Sussex together, he was a great blessing to me, and I am who I am today partially because of my homeboy, DT.

Sussex was a cool spot because of how laid back the staff was. They employed predominantly African Americans so there was a more comfortable vibe there when you had to communicate with the staff, which your average inmate tries to avoid as much as possible, because no matter how cool or understanding an officer may seem, it's never a good look to be in constant communication with the police. This is simply because if someone was to get 'tore off' for drugs, weapons, or whatever, when the inmate population began to investigate as to how the police received such information, you would then become a potential target based on the frequency of your interactions with them (the police). But refraining from interacting with the police at Sussex was easier said than done, because there were so many beautiful corrections officers there.

Based on their background, talking with them was like talking with a chic from around the way. Whatever the name of your hood is, you can put it in the place of 'around the way'. They were just that cool, and sometimes they would even come at you. That happened to me a couple of times while I was there. Of course, those young women I won't name, but basically from the first day I stepped foot on the compound, I attracted the attention of the female officers. And the boldness in which they expressed their interest shocked me a little because I had just spent two and a half years in an Iowa prison where there really was no fraternization going on.

I remember one incident in Fort Dodge where a lady officer was fired for such activities, but at Sussex, stuff like that happened all the time. As I think about it, I'm not really surprised, because in my opinion, it's impossible for a woman to work in this environment where there are so many good looking and intelligent young men, and not be drawn to at least one. Now whether they act on that attraction depends on the individual, but you can trust and believe it's there; the probability is just too high.

Me and my first cell partner there did not get along well; he was a very miserable dude, and often chose to take his misery out on those who were undeserving. While we were in the cell together, he spoke negatively about me behind my back, attempted to sabotage my TV, and he whined and complained about the stupidest of things concerning the cell. The first two offenses were brought to my attention by guys that I barely had a rapport with, but through our limited interaction I believe that they took a liking to me and felt that what was being done behind my back wasn't deserving.

Which they were right, because even though I didn't really care for my cell partner I never deliberately did anything to harm him. So, for him to go behind my back and attempt to destroy the blessings that God had given me was crazy. Normally my response would have been just as crazy, especially prior to my walk with Christ, but thankfully due to the empowerment of the Holy Spirit, I was able to refrain from putting my hands on him. Which Lord knows I wanted to do, because as I've expressed earlier in this book, disrespect is not something that I've ever tolerated. It took everything in me not to beat him bloody. I mean I was so pissed off by what I had heard, and the war between my flesh and spirit was so intense, it brought me to tears. Because on the one hand I wanted so bad to tear this dude's head off, but on the other hand my desire to honor God with my life was just as great.

Up until that point I had never been in such a spiritual struggle. Of course, I told you about the demon that tried to possess me, but this was the first time I was faced with a moral struggle of this magnitude. Do I allow my pride to rise up and beat on its chest, or do I humble myself and allow God to avenge me? In this particular case, humility was the road that I chose, and as opposed to handling the situation violently, I set up a meeting with my counselor to see how I could go about changing cells. She attempted to inquire about why it was I wanted or needed to change cells, but sticking to the code of course, I provided her with no information other than that me and my cell partner just weren't compatible. Seeing how adamant I was about her expediting the move, and I'm sure based on her previous experiences, she agreed to do it and made me promise to be patient and not to take matters into my own hands. So, I gave her my word, which wasn't hard to do because the spiritual war had already been won, I was committed to honoring God.

So, I patiently waited for her to do her thing, and about two weeks later, I was moved to another cell with this cool 'crip' dude by the name of Loco. We got along really well, which is important when you're locked up in a high-level security prison because of how much time you all spend in the cell with each other. On the lower level camps, it's a lot easier to endure having a celly who is in the way because you can minimize your interaction with them. With the camp being so open, and the movement so free, basically the only time you all are forced to cohabitate is during count times and when you all lockdown for the night.

Living with my new celly was a ton of fun, but it was also short lived, due to the fact that a couple of days later, I got hired in the kitchen and moved to the kitchen pod. That was a great blessing, one that if I had allowed my flesh to win in regard to me beating up my old celly, I would no longer have been eligible for. Because outside of the dental shop, the kitchen was the best gig on the compound, and probably if you did a survey, there are some who would call it the best job on the camp. The supervisors were super cool, not to mention all-female, and as long as you worked, they would allow you to eat pretty much what you wanted. Which is a big deal because it helped you save money by not having to go to the canteen every time they offered it. A fact that proved useful to me because after I lost my kitchen job and was moved to the other side of the compound, I still had over a hundred dollars on my books from the checks I had saved.

But here I go again getting ahead of myself, speaking as if my stay in the kitchen pod was brief, when in all actuality I worked there for a little over a year and a half. Far longer than any other job that I'd had prior to, and in spite of the final result, I was proud of how long I had maintained my employment there. My experience in the kitchen was similar to any other I had had at the other places I worked. I always worked hard and therefore gained the favor of all my supervisors, so much so that I was granted as much overtime as I wanted to fatten my check. And I was allowed to eat what I wanted, when I wanted, provided I made a lil extra for the bosses as well. This was a luxury that I knew God had afforded me, and because of that, it wasn't mine to hoard for myself. So, whenever the opportunity presented itself for me to provide a quality meal for those that couldn't find the nerve to ask for certain things themselves, I would do as much as I could to see to it that before the shift ended they were all well fed. And this in turn (as you can probably imagine) earned me the favor of my fellow colleagues, whom I typically worked well with.

I mean, I was the one that would clean extra just so the supervisors wouldn't come down hard on those who didn't work like I did. I would look out when guys were making and drinking wine, and at that time, I wasn't even drinking myself. It was me who would clean up behind them when they either spilled the wine or threw up, and it was never something that I was doing in order to make them feel as if they owed me, instead, I did it out of love. These were my brothers in arms, my comrades, and my fellow coworkers, so anything that I could do to help support them I was willing to do. Trust that I'm not telling you this in order to glorify who I am, but to set the stage so you understand why I was so confused when I ended up getting into a fight with this dude in the gym, one who was also in the pod with me.

Me and him never had any issues prior to the incident in which I speak, and from my perspective, I thought we were pretty cool. He used to write books and I used to always compliment him on his work. I also would go a step further by encouraging him to expand the topics that he wrote about so that he could appeal to a larger audience. Yet in spite of all the conversations we shared and how often he smiled in my face, it appears that all the while there was a hint of jealousy beneath it all. That first surfaced when one night the police came through to search cells and mine was one of the ones that they hit. Our cells were probably like two doors apart, so when they cuffed and pulled me and my cell partner out, he was at the door anticipating the police coming to his cell next, which is something that we all do. So, him being there wasn't even a big deal in and of itself, but the comment that he made while he was standing there was.

I was engaged in a conversation with the guy next door to me inquiring about a remedy for the cold I felt like I was coming down with, and as we spoke back and forth, he (the jealous one) chimed in by saying, "Maybe you should stop working out with your shirt off outside like you're Hercules."

Depending on who you ask that may not sound like much, but when you work out as often and as hard as I do, and someone makes a comment such as he made with malice in his tone then you know that that person is hating. Yet I humbled myself and ignored the comment as if I didn't catch on, because to be honest, when you've been as successful with the ladies as I have been throughout my life, every so often you run into a hater or two who diligently seeks out ways to discredit you. And that's what this situation was all about. I had gained the favor of our supervisors (as I told you earlier) because of how hard I worked, but what I neglected to tell you was that the majority of my supervisors found me attractive as well. They gave me nicknames like Tyrese (the singer), T.O. (the NFL football star) and black Adonis (the Greek sex God) from the very day I stepped foot in the kitchen. The flirting at first was one sided because I was fearful of getting into trouble for crossing the line, like

I said before, not really being used to prison staff coming at me like that. It's funny how on the street if approached in that manner, I would know exactly what to do, but fast forward to me being stripped of my rights and placed in a one-piece jumpsuit, I found myself lost for words.

I bring up the attraction between me and my supervisors because it was brought to my attention after the fight. I learned that envy was part of the reason this individual felt 'some type of way' towards me, all over a supervisor that he liked who enjoyed my company a little more than he was comfortable with. But had he asked, he would have learned that me and hers 'relationship' was strictly platonic, so I was the last person that he needed to worry about. But assumptions were made, and because of that, me and him ended up fighting in the gym one day over both of us attempting to retrieve a loose ball.

At least that's how it appeared, but we all know now that it was way deeper than that. So as the story goes, our pod was scheduled for the gym that day (which was a privilege we would rarely get) so all those that weren't at work went to get a little exercise. And as usual, we picked teams and immediately went to balling because we only had an hour. Me and dude were on the opposite team (not for any particular reason, that's just how it worked out), and somewhere towards the middle of the game, the ball was either stripped or came off the rim, and all those that were in the vicinity made a play on the ball. It just so happened that me and him were the closest ones, and therefore ended up getting there first. He grabbed at the ball, as did I, and as the unwritten rules of engagement state concerning such a play, we wrestled for it until one of us wound up with sole possession. I won this little tug of war match, due to the fact that I was far stronger than this individual, and he ended up falling to the ground in the process. Which isn't something that I intended to have happen, at the same time though I never thought to avoid that outcome; it just comes with the territory as he and I both knew.

But based on the back story I gave you, along with the embarrassment of losing the struggle for the ball, he jumped up and headbutted me. Which (as you can probably imagine) sent me immediately into survival mode, my fist went into autopilot, and before I knew it a flurry of straight jabs were released in the direction of the guy who violated my personal space. He then stumbled and fell, his homeboys came to his aid, and to prevent a sneak attack, I positioned myself with my back against the wall. Assuming that by them seeing that their comrade was overmatched, they would then proceed to jump me. While this was going on though, the police were trying to call for backup. Several times we heard him send out the code (1033) to notify his colleagues that there was a physical altercation taking place. Yet for some reason he couldn't get through, which thankfully afforded those in the pod with us the opportunity to attempt to talk him out of it (calling to get us thrown in the hole.) Due to the persistence of some very persuasive guys, and me and the guy I fought agreeing to drop the issue, the officer allowed us to continue to play.

But in my mind, I wasn't buying the fact that the issue had been squashed, so even while continuing to play, I operated as if the 'beef' remained intact, and at any moment it could go down again. It just seemed too good to be true, because if I were him and he had gotten the better of me, I doubt I would have been able to move on so quickly. The rest of the game went on without so much as an argument taking place (which was strange, but I guess they didn't want to make the officer regret his decision), and once we got back to the pod, me and him talked about it and reaffirmed that we both would put this situation behind us. That was a blessing because most altercations don't end that way, especially not in a level 5 max penitentiary. Those usually don't end until someone sees blood.

So, I know God was in the midst, and further evidence of that was revealed to me when I went to work later that day and had a conversation with the police that tried to call for backup. He came to me and made the comment, "God must really be with you because I did everything I could to force that call through (1033), but regardless of what channel I tried my walky talky would not respond."

The reason he attributed it to God is because he was well aware that I was a man of faith. Pretty much everyone who knew me or had the opportunity to sit down and talk to me, knew that's just kind of how I moved, even often being referred to as a "Jesus freak" by an older gentleman who worked in the kitchen with me because of my passion for Christ. *That* I personally viewed as a compliment because it accurately described the fact that Christ was my everything, and it was becoming more and more evident that within the parameters of this prison I would need him more than ever.

I honestly can't remember what my response was to the statement that the police made, but in my heart of hearts I knew that everything that he said was true. God did intervene and saw fit to spare me from the consequences of my actions. Which would have been (1) me getting thrown in the hole (2) the receiving of a fighting charge (which would have kept me in that particular camp longer) and (3) I would have lost my gig (which would have affected my livelihood). And for His grace I was truly thankful, through that experience God's word was proven to me to be true, that He really does judge the heart.

I harbored no ill feelings towards the guy, but when the situation went down how it did, I did what I felt like I had to do. One of the major reasons I felt so grateful for God allowing my stay to be extended was that it afforded me more time to build with some quality individuals who walked different spiritual paths than my own. We debated, discussed, and shared literature that explained our particular faiths, and I believe that we were made stronger for doing so. I'm well aware of the fact that once these legalistic Christians read that last statement, they'll probably slam the book shut wanting to read no further. Probably parading around the house shouting that we are called to "be ye separated from unbelievers," fearful that somehow in the midst of the discussion of seemingly opposing ideologies an evil spirit may jump on you, possess you, and as a result lead you astray. As opposed to what it did for me, which further solidified my stance and/or faith in Christ.

By the end of our time together, I knew without a shadow of a doubt that I was headed in the right direction, because I had learned that in no other religion had God sent a savior into the world, and once that savior departed, He provided all the necessary help we would need to succeed by way of the Holy Spirit. God is so great, and I was so thankful for him having provided that job for me. Unfortunately, I made a foolish mistake by catching a hundred series charge. Which regardless of what it was for, holds the penalty (among others) of an automatic job removal. That is a rule that they have in place because there are so many inmates looking for jobs, and the prison doesn't have enough to go around. So, having that rule in place keeps the job turnover rate consistent, and they can then say that they at least afforded you a shot.

Not too long after receiving my termination papers, I was moved to the other side of the camp, to a building that had a reputation for being extremely violent. This is where they put their most troubled cases, those that have been to the hole for any number of reasons and have proved to have difficulty adjusting to living amongst the general population. But in spite of all that, I approached that living arrangement the same way I had any other, that "as long as I can pray there, I could stay there." As long as God was with me, I knew that nothing or no one could stand against me, not to mention that I was excited about the opportunity that lay before me to go about the business of winning souls.

So, off I went, and the first cell partner I had was this homosexual by the name of Chesapeake, one of only two cellmates I've had who referred to themselves as gay. He was a good dude, and a straight shooter when it came to anything, especially his sexuality. As soon as I got my stuff together, he came right out with the fact that he was attracted to white men.

My response was, "I'm not into that, but whatever you choose to do in regard to your own life is between you and whatever God you serve."

It's definitely not my place to judge or condemn his actions, but simply to exhibit the love of God through how I treated him. The Bible instructs us not to "show partiality," which means that the same way that I would treat someone whose sexual preferences are more aligned with God's word, is the same way that I should treat those that don't believe as I do. This pod was definitely the wildest pod I had ever been in, yet it was where God did the most in and through me. It started with the fact that I was able to share my testimony with each of my cellmates, which didn't appear to produce any tangible fruit while we were together, but upon parting ways, there were many of them who thanked me for having done so. So, where are they now? I'm not really sure, but I'm leaning on the promise that "God's word shall not return to Him void." And because of that, I believe that something that was said during our time together has taken root along the way (or soon will) and is guiding them in their decision making to this very day.

There was one that showed much promise, and he was the toughest of them all, my main man, Bunchy Carter, who was a well-known member of the 'blood gang.' So much so that he had earned the rank of "GT" (which is the highest rank you can have in that organization), and therefore was granted the option to start his own hood. That is a great honor, one that even I would have considered back in the early part of my bid when I was recruited in Iowa. If I could have turned it into something positive that is, because you know that before Christ, I loved being in charge. And to be honest, to a certain extent I still do, which is something that God is yet working with me on, totally submitting to His will. But me and Bunchy were able to have some deeply spiritual and passionate discussions, and even though he didn't necessarily feel as I did about Christianity, the discussions were respectful and insightful.

You see, Bunchy was a revolutionist that had been taught through his studies of African American literature that Christianity was "the white man's religion," based on the fact that it was used by plantation owners to keep the African slaves subservient, which is a known fact. But my argument was/is that just because someone took the perfect word of God and chose to use it to manipulate those who were uneducated, and therefore, could not read and interpret the scriptures for themselves, does not mean that the word of the Lord at its origin is not still holy. On that fact though, for some reason, we could not agree. Where we did see eye to eye was that it was time for our people, black people, to rise as a whole and take our rightful place in this society. We both believed that our people were created for far more than we had achieved up until that point, but that due to the lies that we've been told about ourselves since we first stepped foot on American soil, and us continuing to operate as though we still believe them, we have settled for living beneath our royal status.

Bunchy inspired me to add to my passion for our people a more in-depth knowledge of what it was that we had actually suffered and how they still oppress us to this day. With the physical barriers having been removed, now the target is our mind. So, when the fight inevitably came, I knew exactly who to attack, how to attack, and why it was that they were to blame. Because our lives here are so brief, it is important that we calculate our steps in a way to ensure that every move we make is moving us towards the change that we desire to see. Shadow boxing is a great workout if you're striving to get physically fit, but in actual life beating against the air is exactly what the enemy wants. And for clarity purposes, I'm referring to the devil when I speak of the enemy, because even though we may be attacked by people, it is technically the 'spirit of the prince of the air' that is guiding their decision making. The Bible speaks of us not being at war against flesh and blood, but against "principalities who control this dark world" (paraphrasing), but at the same time if we are honest, I believe we give the devil way too much credit as it pertains to the temptations that we face and the choices that we make.

The reality of the situation is that we, as a human race, can only be tempted by that which we desire, and because we live in a fallen world, temptation lies around every corner. But at the end of the day, the responsibility remains ours to choose whether we want to conform to the social norms, therefore settling for the status quo, or elevate ourselves by living out the standard set by the creator himself.

Is the devil real?

Absolutely.

Does he desire to destroy you and the plan God has for you?

Most certainly.

Can you resist him under your own strength?

I'm sure you could, for at least a while, but if I were you, I definitely wouldn't risk it.

I mean why would you jeopardize everything that you've worked so hard to obtain by depending on and living only for yourself? Just by believing in your heart and confessing with your mouth that Jesus Christ is Lord, you can be saved, and receive the advocate whose responsibility is to (but not limited to) empower you to withstand all that the enemy sends your way. God not only desires to but will guide you into your destiny. If you allow Him of course. While doing so, He will also provide you with all that you need in order to achieve that which He has set before you, therefore enabling you to receive all the blessings He has in store.

God is great like that. But getting back to the story, Bunchy also introduced me to one of my role models by handing me brother Malcolm X's autobiography, which is still my favorite book outside of the Bible to this day. Malcolm X is absolutely one of my favorite people and someone I strive to emulate, from his discipline in his studies, to his undying commitment to his faith, and the passion he had for black people. For him to go from having a limited education when he first got locked up, being hooked on dope, to transforming himself into one of the most pious and intelligent individuals to ever walk this earth, he is incredibly inspiring to me.

We also discussed other revolutionaries as well, but none affected my life the way that Malcolm did, so much so that I eventually ended up getting a portrait of him tattooed on my leg with one of his well-known phrases "by any means necessary" underneath it.

Me and Bunchy used to wake up like 4 in the morning to work out before breakfast, and yes, there were times when we butted heads, but he was my brother. So, we always worked it out and kept right on doing time. Our time together was brief due to the prison shipping Bunchy to another facility under the excuse that he was a security risk. But I thank God for every minute that we spent together; I really mean that.

CHAPTER 25

4-Building

When I was informed that I was moving to 4-Building, I never could have imagined what God had in store for me. By that time, I was already a faithful member of the Christian community, even though at times when it came to the women there, I did not always conduct myself as a faithful servant should. Yet the Father still saw fit to use me at an extremely high level to minister to those around me, and I assume that based on my faithfulness there in the pod, He deemed me trustworthy enough to steward the whole Christian community in 4 buildings. This was a task that I would have been unqualified for had it not been for the spirit of God flowing through me, providing me with the words to speak and the boldness to speak them. That was God's church, and therefore his people, so in order for me to shepherd them effectively, it was necessary that I totally surrender to His way of doing things.

And of course, that applies to anything that you're attempting to achieve in life. If you want to receive God's best for you in that area, whatever that area is, then it's important for you to seek out his wisdom as to how best to go about fulfilling the task that has been set before you. Only He knows the ins and outs of every situation in your life, and only He can see the potential pitfalls that lay around the corner. So, to avoid such pitfalls, it's imperative that we be sensitive to the Holy Spirit's leading and be obedient to that which He says when He says it. Because delayed obedience can have its consequences as well.

Before the honor of becoming the head pastor over 4-Building, it started in the pod I was in, which speaks to the importance of honoring God right where you are while patiently waiting for him to bring you into your destiny. Me and the Christian brothers came up with the idea to create prayer request slips out of evenly (somewhat) torn notebook paper and slip them under every door in the pod, stating where those who desired prayer could anonymously (or boldly) turn their slips in to receive our attention. Now, of course, prior to this idea, when we used to come together for prayer, we would generally pray for the entire institution, and the prisons all over the world. But by passing out the prayer requests, we were able to allow those who weren't a part of the body of Christ to take a more active role in the healing of whatever the issue was that they were lifting up to the Lord. And they could visibly see us pray over the request. We did it during pod rec. Not for show though; it was just the only time we could all come together, plus it allowed for random walk up requests to take place. When a change occurred concerning their situation, they had a visual to attach to their answered prayer. As a result of that visual, all other explanations for it were dissolved; they knew that God did it, which helped strengthen their faith in Him. It validated in their minds the purpose of the brothers coming together as often as we did.

The most special of times though were the walk-ups, simply because of the bravery that it took for an individual to approach the prayer circle before the eyes of man (their homeboys), when in the eyes of their friends it may have made them look weak or uncool by doing so. On top of that, sometimes they would stay and join hands with us as we prayed, really committing themselves to the process of realigning either their lives or the lives of their family and friends with the perfect will of God. As a result of the obedience that we showed in creating this opportunity for the guys around us, we received plenty of testimonies concerning God answering their prayers, and because of God's goodness, plenty of lives were changed, hopefully forever.

I didn't realize it at the time, but God was slowly elevating me as the leader of this bunch (the Christian brothers in my pod) when it was never my desire to be so, I just enjoyed working hand in hand with my comrades and experiencing the fruit of that work. As I reflect on my life, this has always been the trajectory that my personal relationships have taken, a fact that I expressed earlier, one that my mom pointed out to me when I was younger, and I wasn't ready to receive. But whenever there was something that needed to be done and those around me weren't confident enough in their own abilities to step up and do it themselves, then I would always be the one to whom they'd look, and for that reason, I often found myself forced to "take the bull by the horns" and solve whatever the issue was. It's funny because it wasn't ever because of how highly I thought of myself. I battled many insecurities while growing up, but simply because it needed to be done and no one else would do it. When I was younger, I hadn't heard the term *alpha male*, but as I reflect back on my life, all of my role models could be defined as such, so I've always admired strong, outspoken, confident men. I never viewed myself as such, at least not in the way that those who lacked humility would see themselves in comparison to those around them. I personally always just kind of hoped to blend in, when like King David, Samson, and Joseph in the Bible, God had created me to stand out amidst the crowd or be 'set apart' so to speak.

When I first got to 4-Building, there was a powerful Christian brother whom we referred to as Preacher Man. He was in charge of running the Christian program, and also another brother by the name of Woods, who was the head elder over everything. They both were God fearing, spirit filled individuals who did an incredible job facilitating the service when we wouldn't have any volunteers available to come in from the street. In observing them while leading the service, I learned a lot about what it took to fulfill that role. Although I didn't know that I was in training for that position, and to be honest, nor did I want to be, I was perfectly content with playing the background and serving my Lord in a way that felt comfortable for me. Little did I know that a major shift was about to take place in the Christian prison leadership, and in my life.

CHAPTER 26

Shift

The shift had been prophesied to me just three years prior by a Christian volunteer in Iowa during a Christian revival weekend, and through a vision that God had given me while asleep where I saw an empty pulpit. Of course, at the time of the prophecy, with me being so young in the faith, I basically just smiled and shrugged it off. As for the vision I was divinely given, I didn't have a clue what it meant. I just kind of pocketed it and moved on.

Fast forward to the place where we are now, where the rug was seemingly pulled out from underneath us due to the fact that Preacher Man was awarded his job back in the kitchen and shortly after announced that he would be moving back to 1-Building, therefore leaving 4-Building without an in-house pastor. It seemed like such a devastating blow at the time. We had just become so accustomed to Preacher Man handling everything in regards to the service, and for some reason, the thought of him ever not being able to run the service never even crossed our minds.

But it was as if one day he was there and the next day he wasn't, leaving all of us who were faithful attendees, and who would help out from time to time with the choir and wherever else brother Preacher Man needed us, confused about what the next move should be. So, I felt the need for us to have a meeting amongst the brethren who had worked closely with me in the prayer request operation to see if anyone had any suggestions as to who the leadership should be moving forward. As has been my lot in life, for what seems like my entire life, I saw the look in the eyes of the guys as I posed the question, "What should we do?" The look in their eyes said *whatever it is that you decide, we're going to follow you.* I understood their position on the topic of moving forward, but at the same time did not feel qualified to carry this mantle as the head in-house pastor.

I told them, "It's going to take a collaborative effort to keep the service running as smoothly as it has been."

So, me and a powerful man of God by the name of Sleepy agreed to share the preaching responsibilities. He would teach the Bible study, and I would preach the Sunday service, because there is a big difference between preaching and teaching, and at the time Sleepy was a far better teacher than me. As frightening as it was for us all, and it was definitely frightening for me, we proceeded in faith, trusting God to increase us in every way necessary to ensure that His people (the congregation) were being effectively educated, encouraged, and enlightened through the incomprehensible power of His word.

Surprisingly to me, still believing that we were well over our heads with this one, the transition from brother Preacher Man to us facilitating the Christian service was a rather smooth one. God intervened and showed Himself faithful in a way that I hadn't experienced up until that point, providing us with the boldness, divine insight, and the ability to deliver His message of love, grace, and hope in such a powerful way that the number of attendees actually increased, all while the respect level remained the same. If you've ever been in a max prison, you would understand why that last statement is so important.

Sometimes gang organizations would use these religious services as meeting grounds to discuss topics other than the word of God, and sometimes that would lead to conflict between the Christian community and these organizations because when the 'side talk' would get a little too loud, we viewed that as a sign of disrespect. Of course, regardless of your motives for being there, if it's God's timing for His word to penetrate your heart, then everything else you have going on has to take a backseat to that. Like the word of God says, "Every knee shall bow, and tongue confess that Jesus Christ is Lord," but when your presence during these services becomes a distraction or hindrance to others hearing the Word and enjoying the service, then now we have a problem.

So, several conversations needed to be had, and in certain instances I believe the authorities were asked to get involved, which I took no part in, nor do I condone the involvement of the police in inmate to inmate matters, but to each its own. My solution would have been to keep reminding them (the gang members) to be mindful of the other inmates attending the service and continue to pray that God moves on their heart to want to know more about Him as well, not have them removed from the service for not paying attention or simply talking to their comrades. Because personally, I've been there. I've seen God take a young child who used to go to the back of the church to sleep because I was bored out of my mind, to the point that as a young teen I simply stopped going to church, having no desire to enter into a relationship with Christ, then to as a young adult fall so far from grace to the point of incarceration that most thought that there was no coming back for me, to finally God getting a hold so strong on me that, regardless of how reluctantly, I would assume the responsibility of being the co-pastor of the Sussex 1 Christian service.

I know what it is to be transformed, and I know that it can happen in an instant, so for me to view these gang members as being unsalvageable to me would be extremely hypocritical. Especially since throughout the entirety of my bid, it has been made evident that gang members, those considered to be the worst of the worst in prison, are the individuals to whom I've been called to minister. From the very beginning, the closest relationships that I've had have been with the most violent of the bunch, with them often holding me in higher regard than their superiors in those organizations, referring to me as Brother Mike Nice, aka 'the voice of reason'. These are the individuals that God has consistently used me to pray with, impart wisdom to, and even on occasion lead into a personal relationship with Him. A great pleasure that God has so graciously allowed me to experience, and one for whom I've never considered myself worthy of.

But that's the beautiful thing about my God (and yours too if you choose to believe), regardless of what you've done in your past, or how you view yourself because of it, once you surrender your life to Him, He will from then on only view you through the blood of His son Jesus, and according to the divine purpose that He has for you. So, of course you may not view yourself as worthy in comparison with the glory of the Lord, but God views you as a worthy vessel because of who died for you, and because of what He's placed in, the spirit of God, the Holy Spirit.

So, in keeping up with the story, me and Sleepy co-pastored the church together for about a month until he finally decided to step down due to the pressure that was being applied by the elders of the church because they found out that Sleepy had joined the Bloods (a well-known gang organization). This was a move that he attempted to hide from me at first, obviously because he knew that I wouldn't agree with it, and once we did have a conversation about it, he attempted to justify his choice by claiming that it was the spirit of the Lord that guided his decision. That never really held water with me, but I blindly chose to believe him because I felt like I and the church still needed him. I was afraid of shouldering the load of running the service on my own because, at that time, there wasn't anyone bold enough or well versed enough to take Sleepy's place.

So, when the elders would approach me about having Sleepy step down from his leadership position, I would defend him by highlighting his incredible teaching ability, and speak to how I felt I needed him, to which the brothers would encourage me that I was more than capable of running things on my own. Even though I knew they were right based on how faithful God had shown himself to be during the first transition period, it was hard preaching and teaching twice a week.

When the time came for Sleepy to finally be real with me about it all, I didn't really have much to say other than that it was a pleasure serving with him. It was at this point that it hit me that I had a major decision to make, one that would alter the trajectory of my life. It would either catapult me into my destiny or stagnate my progress. Do I make a run for it like the biblical figure Jonah, ignoring what I know Christ would have me do and potentially wind up in the belly of a metaphorical fish or step out in faith like my man Peter did? I had to trust that as long as I remained focused on Christ, He would continue to give me the ability to minister simply because he had done is thus far. I'm proud to say that I chose the latter and thankfully so because it afforded God the opportunity to prove Himself to be bigger than any of my fears. So, through my trust in Him, I was imparted with the ability to effectively shepherd God's flock for the remainder of my time there, which was roughly a couple of months.

Upon news that I was up for a transfer, God gave me insight into whose hands I was supposed to lead the church, although of course it's always ultimately in God's hands. During those couple of months though I had never felt so fulfilled or useful in my life. Remember this is coming from someone who, from my youth, had had plenty of highs while participating in athletics.

I mean one game was against the high school rival of ours. I specifically remember having played so well and so hard that day and felt such joy from having engaged in such a fierce battle. Having given my all and as a result come out victorious literally brought me to tears. But I repeat, nothing can compare to the complete feeling you receive from answering the call of God on your life and seeing lives forever transformed because of it. Only through surrendering to and living out your divine purpose that we get to experience in the unspeakable joy.

So, it came time for me to pack up for transfer. The procedure goes as follows: they shake your door or call your name over the loudspeaker to notify you that you are needed. Then the booth officer informed you that the property department was prepared for you to bring your belongings to be processed and boxed up. Once you arrived at property with your belongings, they pulled everything out in front of you and counted everything to ensure that you didn't leave anything and so you know what you should have upon arrival at your new facility. Lastly, they tested all electronics to make sure everything worked. The time this process took obviously was determined by the person doing it and how much stuff the inmate being processed had. Once the process was done, the inmate was sent back to the pod with just enough food and hygiene to get through that night.

Depending on how far you had to travel to get to your next institution, you would leave either about 3:00 a.m. that next morning or about 10 a.m. the next day.

Depending on the level of comfortability that you had developed with your celly, those around you, or the routine connected to how the facility operates, the whole transfer process could be bittersweet. On the one hand, I knew I was going to a lower level facility, so that meant more freedom and access to free weights, but to leave my brothers in and outside the church whom I had become extremely fond of, especially when I felt like so much progress was being made, definitely was not easy. So, because of the fondness I had for the guys there, and their fondness for me, the entire day before I was scheduled to leave, I spent it like I only had 24 hours to live.

Making sure that the Spirit led, I sat down with everyone who I had developed somewhat of a relationship with to either give them a few parting words of wisdom, or just to say how much I appreciated the opportunity to have done time with them. Finally, I completed my farewells tour by calling a meeting in which I required all of the Christian brethren to be present. First, to discuss the condition of the church and their responsibilities to it moving forward, and also to express my gratitude for having had the chance to serve with them.

It was definitely an emotional day, but at the same time it was very revealing, because one thing I have learned throughout my journey is that we humans often fail to fully grasp the significance of the moment or season we are in while we are in it. It isn't until that season has passed and you then reflect on it that it all becomes clear as to what it was that God was doing in and through your life. This was the case with me on my final day. I knew that God was working on me and using me to impact the brothers around me, but it wasn't until my final day at Sussex that it became evident just how important the role that God graced me to play in the lives of those I'd been in contact with while I was there.

I found myself in awe by this, and even more confident in the fact that if you are what the Bible calls a willing vessel, then God can use you in greater ways than you could ever imagine, regardless of your age, race, size, or background. All he needs is for you to say yes to His plan, be obedient to the Holy Spirit's guidance, and He will provide for you in abundance whatever it is you think you need to fulfill that plan.

<⟨⟩>

CHAPTER 27

Augusta Correctional

There was nothing of importance that really took place during my transfer; they woke me up about three in the morning like I mentioned was a possibility, and we made a couple stops prior to me reaching my destination. Once I arrived though, I definitely could tell that God had gone before me, and that this was the perfect institution for me to round off my physical, mental, and spiritual maturation process before heading home. God had provided me with a good cellmate who would give me plenty of time to myself if I needed it. He was the same as me in regards to loving to maintain a clean cell, and he was just a real dude, so communicating with him was simple. If we ever felt some type of way about anything going on in the cell, we openly expressed it. All those areas that I just named are vitally important to creating a healthy living arrangement, and the lack of those three courtesies can lead to very heated altercations.

First, it's extremely important that you all respect each other's space while in the cell together and be mindful to give each other space to take care of whatever you all may need to do privately, even if that is to just get away and not see or be bothered by anybody.

Second, is to seek to maintain a clean living environment. This is probably the biggest issue that most cellmates encounter because based on the two individual's upbringing, their definitions of clean may be completely different, or their opinions may differ on how often the cell should be cleaned. But if you so happen to wind up with a cool likeminded celly, then you all would come up with some type of routine where you'd rotate cleaning days. And if not, (I've definitely been there before) you either drive yourself crazy trying to instill in them the importance of cleanliness (which is extremely difficult to do when the individual has been living contrary to that belief), or you do all the cleaning yourself. The latter is the option that I most often have had to choose because rarely was I blessed with a cellmate that likes to and is disciplined enough to clean the way that I do. It even has gotten to the point where when I would get a new cellmate, to avoid any unnecessary drama, I would tell them that they didn't have to worry about cleaning because I would take care of it.

My only request was, "Please do not steal from me, because if you ask, I will gladly give it to you."

I can pretty much cohabitate with anyone except a thief. And thankfully, I never had to, because in prison someone stealing from you is one of the biggest forms of disrespect, one in which even the holiest of men would have a hard time letting slide. If word ever got out about such an offense occurring and it not being handled in a way that the prison population deemed adequate, your cell could turn into a free for all. My family and I work far too hard to acquire the funds that enable me to go to the commissary to retrieve the things that I need, so me allowing someone to violate me in that or any way is completely out of the question.

Last on the list of the three was that cellmates, just like in any living arrangement, should always be open and honest about anything that they think could potentially lead to drama in the cell. If both parties are able to communicate effectively, then nine times out of ten, they will remain on the same page, and therefore be capable of living at peace with one another.

My first cellmate at Augusta was also the second celly that I had who was homosexual, but if you asked him, he probably wouldn't consider himself to be one, which never really made sense to me, but it was also never my place to judge. The only issue I really had with him being my celly was that because we had become friends, I believe some of his boyfriends thought I was capable of being converted too, and that definitely was not the case. Because of that assumption, I had to 'check' a few of the gay guys here just to get them to back off. Depending on how attracted to you they are, they can be very persistent. Nothing was directly said to me that I or anyone standing around might have considered to be too forward or disrespectful, but it was just the look in their eyes when they would see me and the way they would call my name while I was jogging to the yard that would cause me to feel uncomfortable while in their presence.

So, a conversation needed to be had. In love, of course, because I still had to honor God in my dealings with them the same way that I would with anyone else. But situations such as that need to be immediately addressed as to avoid future headaches attached to being mistaken for someone who is actually a part of that lifestyle. Afterwards, though I never had any more problems, and I was able to maintain those associations just in case God wanted to use me to minister in their lives.

Another thing that stood out to me as evidence that God had handpicked this institution for me was the fact that it had the biggest and best weight pit in the state of Virginia. So, with Him knowing how much physical fitness had become and would forever be a part of me, He transferred His favorite son to the biggest playground a fitness freak could ever ask for. Little did I know that fitness would also become the platform that God would use to draw people to me, so that I would have the opportunity to share the gospel. With my love of working out and having just transferred from an institution that rarely let inmates outside (due to them being understaffed), I was outside every chance that was presented to me. Between working out and playing intramural sports, I was able to meet a lot of younger guys at Augusta Correctional and gain their trust, so that whenever they were in need of something, they felt comfortable enough to ask, whether it was a couple of soups to last them until commissary or advice about how to deal with their mate.

Whatever it was that they were dealing with, I quickly developed the reputation of being someone who not only loved sports and fitness, but who deeply cared for them and would do anything to contribute to their success. The favor that God had graced me with led to my developing the reputation as a 'Quality Individual.' When a Muslim guy, named Ali, that I had never met before, came up with the idea to make the Ramadan fast that year, my name was one of the ones brought to his attention to represent the Christian community along with my brother in arms, Don P. Ali's thoughts were that if he could recruit the most levelheaded influential member or members from each gang and or/religion and them have them recruit their counterparts, then he could accumulate a large number of potentially great young future leaders who, if mentored properly, could positively affect the prison culture here. And the hope was that they would take what they learned out into the free world and implement it in their own communities.

So, Ali wisely went about the business of seeking those that he thought to be qualified and sat down one by one to thoroughly explain the vision that God had given him concerning that year's Ramadan. Every person that Ali's spirit led him to approach about a leadership position leaped at the opportunity to contribute to lighting the fire under the next great pastor, politician, business owner, or community activist. This was a frightening proposition to many of us, especially those who had never engaged in public speaking before. It was also a calling by God to use their talent and influence everywhere that he had given us to inspire others to strive for in their lives as well.

I still marvel at what we were able to accomplish that year, the diverse crowd we were able to motivate to participate and the unified bond we were able to create among the inmates. Each message given was well put together and articulated plainly and the willingness of the participants outside of the leadership to lend their gifts to the cause of putting on an incredible talent show was unbelievable. We wanted each participant to leave feeling educated and inspired. We knew that a little fun in between would keep them motivated to return and receive the next day's message. What we were able to accomplish by the grace of God is something that even individuals who had been locked up for three decades or better felt compelled to acknowledge that they had never seen or experienced before. It's sad to say there hasn't been anything like it here since.

As wonderful of a time that month provided for us all, it was short lived. Which is something that I believe has hindered my generation from making that kind of legislative impact that our ancestors did, an unbreakable alliance, regardless of where are from or how much money we made. The organizations we represent simply based on our ethnicity is nonexistent until something tragic happens (i.e., someone being killed by a trigger-happy cop). Even then it quickly fades. The days of viewing one another as brothers and sisters and not enemies or competition must return if we are to take our rightful place in this country. Which is sitting at the same table as those who were born with less obstacles and more opportunities. But unlike our contemporaries who were born with a silver spoon, once we get there, we won't ever regard ourselves as superior nor mistreat those beneath us, because of our lessons of humility that we've received whole enduring our struggle.

<><>

CHAPTER 28

The Divinely Eminent Lifestyle

Once Ramadan was over, my time with Augusta quickly became uneventful. I won a few intramural basketball and softball championships, playing and coaching which was fun. God graced me with a few more speaking engagements, in which those that attended expressed that they were deeply blessed by my authenticity and passion for God, which was incredible to hear.

I also was able by the grace of God to acquire my personal trainer certification, which I am forever grateful to my homegirl Lizzie for footing the bill to make that dream possible. Since my incarceration, fitness has become a major part of my life, it was somewhat of a no brainer. So, when the opportunity presented itself to go about the business of positioning myself to make a career out of a passion, I have to see others obtain their life fitness goals. It turned out to be far more difficult at first. I immediately thought that although I had been consistently reading and studying a wide range of religious and self-help materials, I hadn't been in school or taken a class since 2008 (at least not one that required that much attention to detail), so transitioning back into the classroom was challenging. Thankfully, my desire to get in this particular field was enough motivation to push me through those times when I just didn't feel like doing the required reading.

As usual, God showed up in the moments when I needed Him most, and because of that, ya boy is officially certified to mold and shape individuals into the best version of themselves. It was also at this time that I was in the process of trying to figure out the situation with my heart, deciding whether or not the young lady I was courting at the time was the woman that God created for me. During the time that we dated (while I was incarcerated), all the way up until the time that I finally felt that it was time for us both to romantically move on, "Was she the one?" was the million-dollar question that I constantly went back and forth with a definitive answer. We had history with each other prior to my incarceration, and although the majority of the moments that we shared prior to my imprisonment were strictly centered around us pleasing each other physically, I always viewed her as a good friend. So, when we finally reconnected and the topic came up of us becoming an item, I was hesitant at first because I had never really thought of her in that way.

I also felt that she might not be able to endure the loneliness of being attached to loving someone who is incarcerated. Because naturally and rightfully so, most women want someone there at night to hold on to, someone to go out with, or enjoy those Netflix and chill days. So, for that reason I have never really been a fan of the whole dating someone while locked up idea. I had seen too many guys that I was in jail and prison with who had lost a full head of hair due to the stress attached to not being able to handle the uncertainty of who their woman was spending her time with or giving her body to when on the phone they couldn't get through. I was definitely not interested in doing my time that way.

The Making of a King

But being that not long after us reconnecting I had felt led to apply for a conditional pardon and was extremely confident that my physical freedom would be granted soon, I agreed to attach the tag of boyfriend to what Lizzie and I had going even though I wasn't head over heels with the thought of it. Not that Lizzie wasn't a quality woman, because throughout the time that we dated, she proved to be extremely loving and loyal, but like I mentioned earlier, deep in me was a great deal of skepticism concerning the likelihood that a relationship under these uncommon circumstances could succeed. Despite my skepticism, I threw my entire self into growing our relationship in hopes for that 'Perfect Love' we both would have to look no further for.

That 'Perfect Love Story' that we both sought, we did not find in each other, even though I believe that we both did our best to love each other completely. In most relationships that don't work out, fault can't be attached to either party. We both emptied ourselves so that regardless of the outcome in the end, there would be no regrets. Unfortunately, there were just too many compatibility issues for me to ignore. Issues that I believe would always exist no matter how much time and energy we committed to our relationship, because they weren't simply poor habits that could be changed or that would be eventually grown out of, they were personality traits that, while they by no means made her any less of a great woman, they just didn't mesh well with my personality. To avoid causing her to feel self-conscious about who it was that God created her to be by continuing to complain about things that she was incapable of changing, all the while running the risk of potentially ruining what started out as a great friendship, I eventually got to the point where I strongly believed that there was

148

someone out there that would prove to be a much more suitable companion for her and for me.

So as difficult of a decision as it was for me because I definitely did not want to hurt her, I initiated the conversation that would therefore lead to us parting ways. I assumed that once the relationship was done, that would be the end of me and Lizzie's story. However, despite the disappointment she experienced concerning our breakup, we remained friends and she continued to support me (mentally and emotionally) until God sees fit for me to go home. For that, I will forever respect and appreciate her. One of the major roles that she fulfilled for me at the time was that she handled the operation of my Facebook page, setting it up after a long stint of silence, thus shielding me from basically anyone that was not a part of my immediate family. I felt led in my spirit to do this. It was to be used as an outlet to share my personal writings and also inspirational scriptures and quotes, not really realizing, or putting much thought into how helpful it would be in reconnecting me with my family and friends, most of which I hadn't seen since I was a kid. Now of course, because I'm incarcerated at this time , I don't have internet access to search for those attached to my past, but it turned out that me being able to search wasn't necessary because once I was obedient to the ushering I felt to set up the page, God moved on the hearts of those that He wanted me to be reunited with or that He wanted to receive the message that He has given me.

With the most important of the friend requests that I received being the woman who is now 'The Queen of my Life' and who has turned out to be the 'Woman of my Dreams,' Ms. Stephanie Jane Russotti. She, among many of the friend requests that I'd received, was definitely someone who I never expected to seek me out after we had not spoken in about 15 years. To be honest, at the time that she reached out to me, I was so focused on what I needed to do concerning ending Lizzie and my relationship and fighting to maintain my routine (which helps me to cope with being incarcerated), that the majority of the women attached to my past (especially that far back), I had forgotten about. So much so that when she sent me a message, I was forced to reply by requesting she provide me with a little more information to help jog my memory as to where I should know her from. She graciously provided me with the backstory of how we first met, along with a gorgeous photo of herself. With detailed information, I was immediately taken back in time to a little place I grew up called Lake Park, where the paths of two young teenage kids crossed one hot summer while working to earn a little extra cash. Upon becoming acquaintances, the sparks instantly began to fly, joking and laughing continuously while on the job together, giving each other flirtatious looks, you know, the kind of stuff that boys and girls do when they're feeling each other, but really don't know how to say it. Feeling each other, we most certainly were.

So that little song and dance didn't last long until it transitioned into us hanging out and enjoying each other's company outside of work. Our friendship seemed effortless because we both were always up for a good time, but at the time, that's all it was, a good time. Now let's fast forward about 15 years later to the part that I mentioned earlier that the Holy Spirit placed me on her heart, and as a result, she felt strongly compelled to search the internet to see if I had a Facebook page. Which I also expressed to you earlier, the Holy Spirit led me to create my page for the purposes of ministering the Gospel only a few months prior to Stephanie contacting me. And I did so not knowing, or even assuming, that outside of me helping people, God had the plan in mind to reconnect me with a woman that within the first 2- 3 months of us emailing each other, I would fall head over heels for. This woman pursued me so aggressively that there had to be a Divine Force guiding her decision making, because even though she was unaware when she initiated her search for me that I was incarcerated (to my knowledge), she was a bit shocked, but undeterred.

You can imagine, most people would question whether they had heard God correctly , and even if they didn't second guess themselves, and do believe definitively that they've heard correctly, like Jonah, the seriousness of the trouble that I had gotten myself into would have been enough to drive your average individual in the opposite direction. But thankfully, she was obedient in her pursuit of me to the point that she added herself to my penitentiary email account and thankfully, I was obedient in setting up my personal Facebook account as well as another page called *Truth Be Told*, which gave her the opportunity to preview most of my work. It was access to those writings that gave her a general sense of who I was as a man, and where I was mentally and spiritually in this season of my life, which I believe is crucial to our relationship being where it is. Having this knowledge is what helped assure her that she wasn't crazy for tracking down a felon, but that God did in fact have a plan to use our individual passion for Him to inspire one another to discover the purpose for which we were created.

God had been tugging on her heart, requesting that she allow Him to occupy a greater amount of space in it as He had done for me 11 years prior, isolating me as a way of proving that my relationship with Him is the only one that I absolutely needed. Using my imprisonment as a training ground to prepare me to lead the incredibly strong, beautiful, extremely intelligent woman of God into a future fulfilled with an unprecedented amount of love (for God, from God, and for each other) that requires self-sacrifice and a purpose that reaches across the globe. This is what binds us together, and these are the reasons for which God has reunited us.

But my wife would kill me if I moved on from this story without expressing that our Love Story is without question the greatest Love Story of all times because of the improbability of it, and most importantly the fact that Christ is at the center of it. We've chosen and continue to choose daily to honor each other in the way that we believe Christ would have us to, understanding that everyday won't be perfect, and that it's okay if we disagree as long as we do it respectfully. You would be hard pressed to find a couple who strives to love each other as hard as me and my boo, who are as unwaveringly committed to working through whatever obstacles that the ruler of this world (Satan) may throw our way, and who are as mindful of the fact that our obedience to God in how we treat each other has the ability to guide others to Christ or lead them astray. It can inspire others to work on their relationships or provide them with an excuse/justification for walking away. The realization of how many present and future couples we could potentially help is what motivated us to obey God in creating a relationship devotional that we hope inspires all of our readers to believe that their fairytale love story has already been written by God. And now the only thing that's required of them is to align themselves with God's plan for their lives, so that they find themselves in position to receive their blessing in the form of a life partner. And once the connection is made, we believe that through faith in God and the adherence to His Divine Word, applying it to your personal life and home life, you are assured to experience what me and my wife like to call the Divinely Eminent Lifestyle.

So, yes I am extremely grateful for the woman that God has so lovingly provided for me, because I am a far greater man for having her as my co-CEO in life. To be honest, having the privilege to love her and be loved by her still feels sort of surreal, like when you find yourself reflecting on your life with a huge smile on your face wondering, *how did I get so lucky?* God has been so good to me, and so has she.

My prayer is that I prove to be consistently qualified to lead her and our family into the vision that God has given me, and therefore never cause her to regret the fact that she chose me as her King.

About the Author

Michael B. Brown serves as a leader and mentor to young inmates at a correctional institution in Craigsville, Virginia. He was a top recruited high school football player who received a full athletic scholarship to Virginia Tech in 2003. It was during this time that he began a downward spiral which led to his incarceration. Although he shied away from being viewed as a role model prior to his incarceration, it became apparent throughout the years that he was destined for leadership. This humbling experience led him back to a personal relationship with Jesus Christ. God continued to put him in leadership roles where young men would look to him for guidance and direction. He would pray with them and advise them in a way that he believed God approved of. This led to him becoming a lead minister at one of the correctional institutions and the 'go to' guy when someone needed encouragement. Today he is a fiancé, father, and an up and coming bestselling author.

www.ingramcontent.com/pod-product-compliance
Lightning Source LLC
Chambersburg PA
CBHW051725040426
42447CB00008B/982